Contents

MINUTE
GUIDE TO
Internet
Assistant for
Word

J. Michael Roach

A Division of Macmillan Computer Publishing
201 West 103rd Street, Indianapolis, Indiana 46290 USA

© 1995 Que Corporation

International Standard Book Number: 1-56761-616-X
Library of Congress Catalog Card Number: 94-074506

97 96 95   8 7 6 5 4 3 2 1

Interpretation of the printing code: the rightmost number of the first series of numbers is the year of the book's printing; the rightmost number of the second series of numbers is the number of the book's printing. For example, a printing code of 95-1 shows that the first printing of the book occurred in 1995.

Publisher: *Roland Elgey*
Vice President and Publisher: *Marie Butler-Knight*
Publishing Manager: *Barry Pruett*
Editorial Services Director: *Elizabeth Keaffaber*
Managing Editor: *Michael Cunningham*
Development Editor: *Heather Stith*
Production Editor: *Kelly Oliver*
Manuscript Editor: *San Dee Phillips*
Technical Editor: *Christopher Denny*
Book Designer: *Barbara Kordesh*
Indexer: *Kathy Venable*
Production Team: *Anne Dickerson, Maxine Dillingham, Chad Dressler, Daryl Kessler, Bob LaRoche, Erika Millen, Kaylene Riemen, Kris Simmons, Tim Taylor, Michael Thomas, Scott Tullis, Jody York*

Screen reproductions in this book were created by means of the program Collage Complete from Inner Media, Inc., Hollis, NH.

Printed in the United States of America

Introduction

Imagine a world where thousands upon thousands of documents are available electronically to millions upon millions of people. That world is here, today—the World Wide Web.

Personal computers, for the most part, are about the creation of documents, all kinds of different documents: text, spreadsheets, databases, pictures, graphics, and charts. With most word processors, you can create documents that contain all of these types of information. These documents are meant to be seen by or used by someone other than the person who created them; sharing documents is the main thrust of modern computing. Then there's this thing called the *information superhighway*. This highway is under construction even as we speak, and the purpose of this highway is sharing documents.

Many businesses, large and small, are using the World Wide Web for advertising, customer service, marketing, and countless other creative strategies. Millions of people throughout the world use the Web for personal pleasure, research, or the opportunity to meet interesting people. This technology has caused the largest explosion in the history of personal computing.

If you're uncomfortable with the Internet, consider reading the *10 Minute Guide to the Internet*, by Peter Kent.

Welcome to the *10 Minute Guide to Internet Assistant for Word*

Because most people don't have the time to sit down for a few consecutive hours, this book focuses on the fundamentals (you will not learn everything about the program) of using Microsoft Internet Assistant. You can learn each feature or concept in a single lesson that takes 10 minutes or less to complete.

Straightforward, easy-to-follow explanations and numbered lessons get you up and running with Internet Assistant quickly by teaching by example. You'll see step-by-step directions that tell you exactly what to type, where to click, what keys to press—how to be productive with Internet Assistant right now.

Who Should Use the *10 Minute Guide to Internet Assistant for Word?*

The *10 Minute Guide to Internet Assistant for Word* is for anyone who:

- Needs to learn Internet Assistant quickly.

- Feels overwhelmed by the complexity of Internet Assistant or the Internet.

- Wants to find out quickly whether Internet Assistant will meet his or her needs.

- Wants a clear, concise guide to the most important features of Internet Assistant.

What Is Internet Assistant?

Internet Assistant is a small add-on utility for Microsoft Word for Windows 6.0a. After installation, Word becomes a complete Internet browsing station. Internet Assistant gives Word the capability to retrieve documents from the Internet and display them on your screen. After you install Internet Assistant, you get the following features:

- Internet browsing support for the World Wide Web, FTP, and Gopher.

- Powerful, easy-to-use features and tools for creating your own Internet documents.

- Convenient converters for converting Internet documents to Word format.

- Much, much more.

How to Use This Book

The *10 Minute Guide to Internet Assistant for Word* consists of a series of lessons, ranging from basic startup to a few more advanced features. It also explains about the Internet and the process of writing HTML documents.

If you've never used the Internet before, start with Lesson 1 and work forward at your own pace. If you're familiar with the Internet, you may feel comfortable skipping the first few lessons. The last few lessons deal with advanced features and give the advanced user an opportunity to become more familiar with Internet Assistant on a technical level.

Although you can use this book as a tutorial, it will also serve as a handy reference tool even after you become familiar with using Internet Assistant. Refer to this book if you forget how to perform a certain task or if the Help file doesn't contain a thorough reference.

Icons and Conventions Used in This Book

The following icons have been added throughout the book to help you find your way around:

Timesaver Tip icons offer shortcuts and hints for using the program efficiently.

Plain English icons define new terms.

Panic Button icons appear where new users often run into trouble.

The following conventions clarify the steps you perform:

On-screen text	Any text that appears on-screen appears in **bold type**.
What you type	The information you type appears in bold color type.
Press Enter	Keys you press (or selections you make with the mouse) appear in color type.
Key+Key Combinations	When you need to use a two-key combination to enter a command (for example, "Alt+X"), press and hold the first key, and then tap the second key.

Trademarks

All terms mentioned in this book that are known to be or are suspected of being trademarks or service marks have been appropriately capitalized. Que Corporation cannot attest to the accuracy of this information. Use of a term in this book should not be regarded as affecting the validity of any trademark or service mark.

Lesson

Understanding the Internet and the World Wide Web

In this chapter, you'll learn about the Internet and how it started. You'll also learn about the World Wide Web and why it has become so popular.

What Is the Internet?

The *Internet* is an extremely large and complex—yet fast and powerful—network of millions of machines that can communicate with one another. All kinds of people and organizations own these computers:

- Large universities maintain computers connected to the Internet. Most of the computers are open to the public on the Internet. Many universities keep archives of special studies and research available on the Internet.

- Government agencies maintain systems on the Internet as well. One of the more popular agencies is the Library of Congress, which maintains an extensive database that Internet users can access.

- Large companies such as IBM, Intel, Microsoft, and many others maintain systems on the Internet. Some of these companies have certain areas accessible by the general public.

- Small companies are learning about the advantages of maintaining systems on the Internet, as well. Many small companies are experimenting with customer service, sales, and even marketing via the Internet.

- Private individuals are also enjoying the challenge of connecting their machines to the Internet. Some are connecting from home, but many are students at colleges and universities that have Internet access.

The beauty of the Internet is that most of the communication occurs over the phone lines, which makes it very cost effective. Most of the major backbones of the Internet consist of fiber-optic cables known as T1 and T3 lines. The fiber-optic links allow for great speed and reliability across long distances. The phone company has already gone to the expense of laying the physical wire (which is one of the most expensive areas of networking); all you have to do is pay for the service.

The Internet consists of all kinds of things to do and all types of information. You can find discussion groups, electronic mail, live conversation, file archives, and much more.

The main reason there is so much to do on the Internet is simple: there are no governing agencies, no laws, and no controlling boards that dictate how you can use the Internet. There are, however, "standards boards" that provide "suggestions," but it is not necessary for you to follow them.

I like to think of the Internet as the only real example of anarchy that works. The only reason the Internet can continue the way it does is by mutual agreement of millions of people with the same goal: the fastest and most powerful method for communication among people all over the world.

These millions of people can communicate with one another in a variety of ways. Here are a few:

- **Telnet**   Terminal emulation link network. Telnet allows you to connect to a remote system and operate it from your computer.

- **FTP**   File transfer protocol. A program that allows you to connect to a remote system and transfer files to and from that system. Lesson 7 explains how you can use Internet Assistant with FTP.

- **Gopher**   A browsing system that gives you access to resources linked together by a menu system. For the most part, the World Wide Web is replacing this technology. Lesson 8 explains how you can use Internet Assistant with Gopher.

- **WWW**   World Wide Web. A complex collection of graphical documents stored on thousands of computers around the world. Each document connects to other documents via hypertext links. I'll explain hypertext links in the next section.

- **WAIS**   Wide Area Information Search. A complex searching program (called a *search engine*) that locates information resources on the Internet by means of a scoring system. Each resource is "weighted" based on the search criteria. The WAIS server then presents you with the results of the search.

- **e-mail**   Electronic mail. A method of sending typed notes or letters across a computer network. Some companies have e-mail that works within the company. You can also use the Internet to send e-mail.

- **Usenet**   A collection of discussion groups (usually called *newsgroups*) stored in a central location. Newsgroups are similar to message areas on BBSs (bulletin board systems), forums on CompuServe, or the employee bulletin board at work on which you can post items of interest for others to read. You can connect to a machine and read through the articles in a specific newsgroup or contribute new articles to that newsgroup.

What Is the World Wide Web?

The World Wide Web is a large collection of documents stored on the Internet. Each of these documents link to other documents with a technology called *hypertext*. You may not recognize the term, but I'll bet you've used hypertext before. If you have made that last-resort reach for the Help menu in a Windows program, then you are familiar with hypertext. Remember those little green words? Each time you click on a green word, the program takes you to a related "page" or "document." That's hypertext.

With the World Wide Web, each document can "point to" or "take you to" countless other documents on the Web. The other documents can exist on the same computer or on a different computer—even one on the other side of the world. Traveling from one document to another in search of information is known as "browsing the Web" or "surfing the Net."

To browse the Web, you need a *Web browser*, which is a piece of computer software that requests documents from other computers. The most remarkable part of the system is the method for locating these documents.

Each document on the Web is identified by a *Uniform Resource Locator*, or *URL* (pronounced "earl"). The URL contains the *domain name* of the computer and the path and file name of the document. This small piece of information can be embedded into a document or typed in by the user. An embedded URL is known as a *link* or an *anchor*; it usually appears in blue and (sometimes) under-lined text. This sets it apart from the rest of the text. You can click on any blue underlined word to see another document, or *Web page*.

Domain Name A naming scheme used by the Internet to allow humans to easily identify a specific computer. Each domain name represents a numerical address. A separate computer translates the domain name into the numerical address (known as an *IP address*) for you—similar to how the phone book converts a person's name into a phone number.

Most Web users will start with a *home page*. These home pages typically contain links to many other subject-related documents. In any case, the trick is to find a good place to start, and then you can continue to browse from there.

Home Page The term *home page* can refer to the starting document used by a Web browser or the starting-points document on a Web site.

Web Site A computer that contains a collection of Web pages.

Web documents usually contain text that is formatted based on special codes that are embedded into the docu-ment. This differs from traditional forms of document transfer (such as faxing) where a graphical image of the document transfers from one system to another. This graphi-cal (or bit-mapped) form of transferring documents is extremely time-consuming. Since Web documents consist mainly of text, the transfer time is significantly reduced. Lesson 10 explains the Web document language (HTML) in greater detail.

In addition to text, you can include the following kinds of material on your Web page:

- **Pictures**   A picture or graphic displayed within a document is known as an *inline graphic*. You can create an inline graphic by saving the picture in a special format and transferring the file name and instructions about where you want it to be placed in your document. After the text loads, the graphics transfer begins. The browser downloads each picture, decodes it, and displays it on your screen with the rest of the document. Lesson 13 explains how to create inline graphics.

- **Links to sound and motion-video files**   If the file you link to your Web page is associated with an application other than the Web browser, the browser will run that application with the down-loaded file. For example, I can include a *.WAV file* of my voice in my home page. If you clicked on the link that points to that .WAV file, your browser would download the file and pass it to a program that plays the sound. Lesson 12 explains how to create hypertext links.

    .WAV File   A compressed file that contains a digitized sound or recording.

- **Fill-out forms**   Fill-out forms give the user of a Web document the ability to send information to the *server*. You can use forms to register software, request information, and even order pizza. Many Web sites contain forms that you can use to search for information at that Web site. You can also use forms to create custom Web pages on the fly.

Companies large and small have created Web sites complete with form support to enhance their competitive edge and offer unprecedented levels of technical and consumer support services. Many also provide megabytes of information for customers and customers-to-be. Lesson 15 explains how to create fill-out forms.

Server   A computer on the Internet that stores documents or information and runs a program that communicates with remote computers to share information. A server that runs software for WWW users to connect to is called a *Web server*.

In this lesson, you learned about the Internet and how you can use it. You also learned about World Wide Web and why it has become so popular. In the next lesson, I'll explain how Microsoft Internet Assistant makes it easier to use the Internet—the World Wide Web in particular.

Lesson

What Is Internet Assistant?

In this lesson, you'll learn about Microsoft Internet Assistant and what it can do for you.

Internet Assistant is an add-on for Microsoft Word for Windows. If you are a registered user of Word for Windows, you are legally allowed to use Internet Assistant at no additional charge.

Add-On A program, utility, or software package feature that doesn't ship with the product but is included in the purchase price of the software license. Add-ons are usually produced after the software is finished. Although Internet Assistant is provided at no additional charge to registered users of Microsoft Word, most add-ons are available for a small license fee. (See the "Locating Internet Assistant" section in Lesson 4 for more information.)

The main purpose of Internet Assistant is to enable Word users to easily share information via the World Wide Web. The following sections explain the three main ways Internet Assistant does this.

Creating and Editing HTML Documents

If you've ever spent time writing HTML (Web language) documents before, you know that it can be painstaking and time-consuming. You have to place each command within the text one character at a time. If you wanted to specify a phrase as a header, you'd have to type this line:

<H1>This is a header</H1>

HTML   HyperText Markup Language. Web documents are composed using this language. Internet Assistant automatically generates the code for this language, saving users countless hours in Web page development.

Although it isn't a huge pain, one problem persists: the author of an HTML document has no idea what the finished document will look like when viewed with a Web browser. To give you an idea of what's involved, here's the process I go through when I create new HTML documents:

1. Type in the new header or paragraph.

2. Type in the HTML code on either side to indicate headers or paragraph text.

3. Save the file.

4. Load the file into a separate Web browser to see what my changes look like.

5. Repeat this process for each major change I make.

This method of creating HTML documents works well, but it takes a lot of time. Internet Assistant uses the built-in styles from Microsoft Word to make HTML document composition easier. For example, instead of typing the actual HTML code, you can select **Header** from the list of styles.

The main advantage to Internet Assistant is that it incorporates all the advantages of a full-featured word processor into your HTML editor. For example:

- WYSIWYG (What You See Is What You Get) formatting in a graphical environment so you can see what your HTML will look like while you're creating or editing it.

- Spell checkers and grammar checkers.

- A point-and-click graphical environment with helpful icons (small pictures) to automate frequent or complicated tasks.

- Document converters that enable you to use existing documents as HTML documents with a single mouse click.

HTML Editor   A software package or utility designed to assist you in writing HTML documents. Although you can write HTML documents in any text editor or word processor, an HTML editor usually contains some extra features that make your job a bit easier. Internet Assistant essentially turns Word into a full-fledged HTML editor.

Plain English

Never before has creating HTML documents been this easy. Plus, Internet Assistant allows you to browse the Web from your word processor and cut documents right off the Internet and paste them into your own document.

Internet Assistant provides you with templates and document converters that make creating HTML documents as easy as creating a business letter or interoffice memo.

Internet Assistant also contains special formatting tools that make creating HTML documents a breeze; they work just like the ones you've been using for your regular Word documents. Internet Assistant gives you one-click access to the following functions:

- Left- or right-justified text

- Centered text

- Bold, italic, and underline

- Numbered and bulleted lists

- Indented paragraphs and lists

I'll discuss HTML documents in more detail in Lessons 10 and 11.

Browsing the Web

The first major step in launching the Internet with non-technical users was a program called Mosaic®, produced and published by the National Center for Supercomputing Applications (NCSA). Mosaic was the first popular Web browser to take advantage of the capabilities of graphical operating systems such as Microsoft Windows, System 7.5 (Macintosh), and X Window (a graphical UNIX operating system).

The biggest advantage of Mosaic and other graphically oriented Web browsers (such as Netscape, another popular Web browser) is point-and-click access to the Internet. In the past, users had to have excellent technical skills to use the Internet. With the modern Web browser, technology that has been available for over two decades is now at the fingertips of the nontechnical user.

The next big step in bringing the Internet to the masses is Microsoft Internet Assistant. With this program, not only can the nontechnical person browse the Web, he can also create documents for it. Although Internet Assistant has all the functionality of a Web browser, it is important to realize that Internet Assistant is not designed to be the greatest Web browser. As a matter of fact, Internet Assistant is rather slow and sluggish as a Web browser. It is, however, the most useful tool available for creating and editing HTML documents. Its Web browsing facilities give you the ability to download Web documents and cut and paste them into your own HTML or Word documents. If you plan to create your own Web pages to establish your own Web site on the Internet or if you want to have the ability to link your Word documents to other network resources (such as Web pages and Gopher menus), then Internet Assistant is the tool for you.

Surfing the Internet

Browsing the Web is only one of the many things you can do on the Internet. In order to truly surf the Net, a user must have many different tools available. Other popular tools to use on the Internet are FTP and Gopher; fortunately, Internet Assistant provides support for those tools. I'll introduce FTP and Gopher in Lessons 7 and 8.

In addition to these tools, Internet Assistant also contains a full set of tools and features that make your Web browsing experience simple and easy:

Internet Toolbar   An additional toolbar that appears when you enter Web Browse view. This toolbar has buttons that allow you to access most of the features of Internet Assistant.

Favorites Document   A comprehensive list of Web documents that you enjoy. Each time you see a Web page you like, you can add it to your Favorites list.

History   A list of documents that you've browsed during the current session. Simply click on the title of the document that you want to review, and it reappears. You can view this list at any time during your Web browsing session.

Home Page   Microsoft has included a sample starting-points document that resides on your hard disk. This page provides links to a great selection of documents so you can start browsing the Web immediately.

Don't worry if you're still a little overwhelmed. I'll explain each one of these tools to you as I take you through a tour of Internet Assistant in Lesson 5.

In this lesson, you learned what Internet Assistant can do for you. In the next lesson, I'll explain what you'll need before you can access the Internet with Internet Assistant.

Lesson

What You Need to Use Internet Assistant

In this lesson, I'll explain what type of system you need to have in order to use Internet Assistant. I'll also explain TCP/IP, SLIP, PPP, and other methods of connecting to the Internet.

Getting an Internet Service Provider

To get the most out of Internet Assistant, the first thing you need is an Internet connection. To get this, you need an *Internet service provider*. If you don't want to connect to the Internet, you can still use Internet Assistant to create HTML documents, but you won't be able to retrieve documents from other computers. In this case, you won't need TCP/IP software, either. If you want to connect to the Internet (or if you'd like a quick refresher course), continue reading.

Internet Service Provider   A company that provides access to the Internet via a phone line or dedicated connection.

An Internet service provider maintains a computer that connects to the Internet. This company, in turn, sells you access to that computer (usually for a monthly fee) and thus, access to the Internet. Your computer sends Internet data through a modem or network interface card (located inside the computer, in most cases), which connects to the other computer via telephone lines (with a modem) or a cable (with a network card). The other computer sends that data across the Internet. Also, any data that is supposed to come to you is picked up by the other computer and sent to you over the wire.

To obtain a list of Internet service providers, you can usually check your Yellow Pages under Computing. If you don't find a listing that sounds like an Internet service provider, call some of the computer retail stores. They should be able to point you in the right direction. The Internet service provider will give you detailed instructions on how to connect.

Getting the Right TCP/IP Software

TCP/IP stands for two different *protocols* (computer communication languages) the Internet uses. TCP is the Transport Control Protocol. TCP assures that there are no errors in your data. It also keeps track of the other computer you're talking to. IP is the Internet Protocol. IP assures that data goes to the right place.

In most cases, your Internet service provider can supply you with TCP/IP software. However, you may want to purchase your own. The important thing is to make sure your TCP/IP stack is *WinSock compliant* (will work with Windows). Most packages will include this fact in the documentation or on the outside of the box. If you're still unsure, contact the vendor or a salesperson in the store.

To make it a bit easier, I've included a short list of common TCP/IP stacks that are WinSock compliant:

- Trumpet WinSock version 1.0 or greater.

- PCTCP from FTP software. Current version is 4.0.

- NetManage from Chameleon Software.

- Novell's LAN WorkPlace for DOS.

- Microsoft TCP/IP 32 from Windows for Workgroups (also known as Wolverine).

This is not a complete list, but these are the most popular and they all work quite well.

Getting the Right Connection

Most Internet users use a direct connection if the computer is at work or at school. Many companies, colleges, and universities have Internet access direct from the local network.

Most users who need Internet access from home use a modem and call into a Internet service provider with a SLIP or PPP connection.

SLIP   Serial Line Internet Protocol. An older method of using the Internet over a modem (or a serial cable). Most Internet service providers allow SLIP access.

PPP   Point-to-Point Protocol. A newer, but less common method of using Internet over a modem. PPP automatically takes care of much of the setup, and, therefore, is much easier for nontechnical people to use.

SLIP or PPP?   When given a choice between SLIP and PPP, you should almost always choose PPP. However, be sure that your TCP/IP stack supports PPP, as well. Ask your service provider for help if you're unsure about which connection you need.

SLIP and PPP are only used over a modem or serial cable. If you're using the Internet from work or school and your PC is connected to the network with a network card, you won't need to worry about SLIP or PPP. Some other issues arise when using the Internet over a network card. You should be sure that you have the necessary drivers (programs) to run TCP/IP over your network card. Unfortunately, I could write a 300-page book on this topic alone; I can only give so much guidance. (If you really want to know about Internet connections, read *The Complete Idiot's Next Step with the Internet*, by Peter Kent.) Here are a few tips, though:

- Know who made your network card and how to contact them via phone or fax. They should be able to answer most of your questions.

- Know who wrote your TCP/IP software, as well. Chances are, they've run into the same situation during their own testing process. Know how to contact them via phone or fax.

Meeting the Basic System Requirements

In order for Internet Assistant to work properly, you'll need a system with the following:

- An Intel 386 microprocessor or higher.

- An installed copy of MS-DOS version 3.0 or greater.

- Microsoft Windows version 3.1 or greater, Microsoft Windows for Workgroups version 3.1 or greater, Microsoft Windows NT, or Microsoft Windows for Pen Computing.

- An installed copy of Microsoft Word for Windows 6.0a or greater.

- At least 6M of RAM (I recommend at least 8M).

- At least 2M of free hard disk space on the same drive as Word for Windows.

- A Microsoft mouse or compatible pointing device.

- A modem and a telephone line or a network connection to the Internet.

- Internet service provider.

If you're not sure which version of Word you have or whether your system meets some of the other requirements, follow these steps:

1. Start Word for Windows.

2. Pull down the Help menu and select About Microsoft Word. The top of the About Microsoft Word window that appears lists the version of Word you have installed, as shown in Figure 3.1.

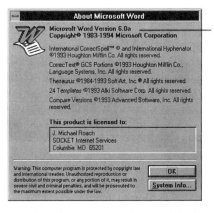

Look here to see which version of Word you have installed.

Figure 3.1 The About Microsoft Word dialog box.

3. To find out other system information (such as your Windows version, DOS version, or available hard disk space), click the System Info button in this window to display the System Info window.

4. Click Close to close the System Info window.

5. Click OK to close the About Microsoft Word window.

If you still have questions about whether your system meets the requirements, contact your computer reseller or your documentation for help in determining your current setup.

Getting the Correct Version of Word

If you are running Microsoft Word for Windows but it isn't version 6.0, you need to purchase an upgrade from Microsoft. Upgrades are also available in retail stores. Mine cost about $130.

If you are running Microsoft Word for Windows 6.0 but not 6.0a, you can download the Word 6.0a patch from Microsoft.

> **Patch**   A small program that updates or changes another program. Patches usually fix bugs (minor program flows) or add features.

Plain English

If you have access to Internet FTP (File Transfer Protocol) and you know how to use it, you can get the patch from the Microsoft FTP site. To get the patch over the Internet, follow these steps:

1. Start your FTP client.

2. Connect to ftp.microsoft.com (198.105.232.1).

3. Use anonymous as your login ID.

4. Use guest@ (or your e-mail address if you have one) as your password.

5. Change to the /softlib/MSLFILES directory.

6. Download the file called word60a.exe.

To download the patch from the Microsoft Download Service:

1. Start your communications software.

2. Set your port settings to N81 (no parity, 8 data bits, 1 stop bit). Refer to the manual of your communications software if you're not sure how to do this.

3. Set your terminal emulation to ANSI. Again, refer to your communications software manual if you don't know how to do this.

4. Dial 1-206-936-6735. When the connection is made, you see a screen similar to the one shown in Figure 3.2.

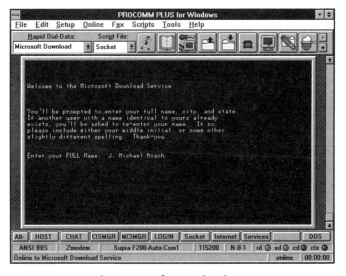

Figure 3.2 The Microsoft Download Service main screen.

5. Enter your full name at the FULL Name prompt.

6. Press 2 to select File Index from the Main menu.

7. Press 2 to select Word, Excel, Office and Multiplan.

8. Press 2 to select Word for Windows.

9. Press S to stop the file listing.

10. Press P and then press **Enter**. You will see a list of file transfer protocols.

11. Choose a file transfer protocol (ZModem in most cases).

12. Press D and press Enter.

13. Type **WORD60A.EXE** when prompted for a file name.

It's Not Working! If you have any trouble with these steps, you can reach Microsoft Word Technical Support at (206) 462-9673 between 6:00 a.m. and 6:00 p.m. Pacific Time, Monday through Friday.

To install the patch:

1. Switch to File Manager.

2. Select File Search from the menu bar.

3. In the Search dialog box, type **WORD60A.EXE** and press Tab.

4. Type C:\ and press Enter. The File Manager will search your entire hard disk for the file.

5. In the Search Results window, highlight (click once) WORD60A.EXE.

It Didn't Find It   If File Manager did not find the file, it's possible that you saved it on a drive other than C:. If that is the case, repeat the above steps and substitute C: with the drive letter you are using.

6. Double-click WORD60A.EXE to install the patch.

In this lesson, I explained what type of system you need to have to use Internet Assistant. I also explained TCP/IP, SLIP, PPP, and other methods of connecting to the Internet. In the next lesson, I'll take you step by step through installing Internet Assistant on your computer.

Lesson

Installing Internet Assistant

In this lesson, I'll take you step-by-step through installing Internet Assistant on your computer. I'll also help you make the best choices for your machine during the setup process.

Internet Assistant is quite picky about the system on which it resides. For this reason, system requirements are more of an issue than they might normally be. I covered most of the requirements in the previous lesson. If you haven't read through them, I recommend that you take a quick look at Lesson 3.

Locating Internet Assistant

You can find Internet Assistant in a number of different places. To ensure that you get the most recent copy, I recommend obtaining it from one of the following sources: the Microsoft FTP server, the Microsoft Download Service, or the Microsoft World Wide Web site. The following sections explain how to do this.

Downloading Internet Assistant from the Microsoft FTP Server

To download Internet Assistant from the Microsoft FTP Server:

1. Start your FTP client.

2. Connect to ftp.microsoft.com (198.105.232.1).

3. Change to the /deskapps/word/winword-public/ia directory.

4. Download the file called wordia.exe.

Downloading Internet Assistant from the Microsoft World Wide Web Site

If you have a Web browser already, you can download Internet Assistant from the Microsoft World Wide Web site:

1. Start your Web browser.

2. Enter the following URL:

> http://www.microsoft.com/pages/
> deskapps/word/ia/default.htm

A page from the Microsoft Web site appears, as shown in Figure 4.1.

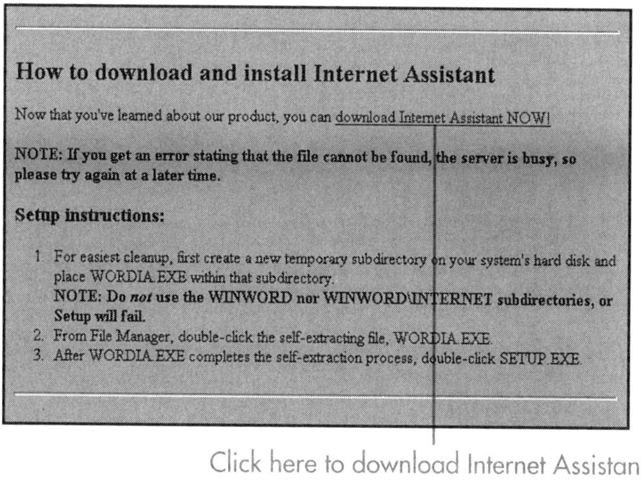

How to download and install Internet Assistant

Now that you've learned about our product, you can download Internet Assistant NOW!

NOTE: If you get an error stating that the file cannot be found, the server is busy, so please try again at a later time.

Setup instructions:

1. For easiest cleanup, first create a new temporary subdirectory on your system's hard disk and place WORDIA.EXE within that subdirectory.
   NOTE: Do *not* use the WINWORD nor WINWORD\INTERNET subdirectories, or Setup will fail.
2. From File Manager, double-click the self-extracting file, WORDIA.EXE.
3. After WORDIA.EXE completes the self-extraction process, double-click SETUP.EXE.

Click here to download Internet Assistant.

Figure 4.1   A page from the Microsoft Web site. Yours may look slightly different.

---

3. Look for the How to Download Internet Assistant header.

4. Click the download Internet Assistant hyperlink. A new page will appear.

5. On the new page that appears, click the download Internet Assistant hyperlink.

6. If you're not sure where your Web browser saved the file, you can locate the file by typing **dir wordia.exe /s** from the root directory of your hard disk.

Extracting the Setup Files

It's a good idea to keep your hard drive relatively uncluttered. Since you won't need WORDIA.EXE after everything's installed, I recommend creating a directory called \WORDIA on the same drive as Word for Windows. Then copy or move WORDIA.EXE into that directory.

WORDIA.EXE is a compressed archive of the actual setup files. Therefore, you need to execute WORDIA.EXE first to extract the setup files. The archive is self-extracting, so all you need to do is run this file by double-clicking its name in File Manager. The extracted files will be in the same directory as WORDIA.EXE.

Running the Setup Files

To run the setup files and install Internet Assistant:

1. Run SETUP.EXE. (From File Manager, select File Run.) You should see the Run dialog box.

2. Type \wordia\setup and press Enter.

3. Read the introductory dialog box and click OK.

4. Read the license agreement (you'll have to click Continue to read all the pages). If you agree with the terms of the license, click Agree. The dialog box shown in Figure 4.2 appears.

Click to continue.

Click to change the installation directory.

Figure 4.2   Click the Continue button to install Internet Assistant.

5. By default, Internet Assistant is installed in a subdirectory of your Word for Windows directory (in most cases C:\WINWORD\INTERNET). Unless this is a problem, leave the default. If you'd like to change this, click Change Directory and type in the new directory. When you're ready to proceed, click the Continue icon.

6. At this point, Setup will ask you if you want to install the Internet Browsing portion of Internet Assistant. If you have Internet access, choose Yes. If you don't have Internet access, choose No and you can still use the HTML editor function of Internet Assistant. Setup will copy the files and update your system files to reflect the additional features of Internet Assistant.

7. When the file copying process is complete, Setup will ask if you want to start Word. If you're ready to begin, click Launch Word. If, on the other hand, you're not all that excited about it, click Exit and continue with the lessons later.

Deleting the Setup Files

When you finish installing Internet Assistant, you can delete the setup files to save hard disk space. They take up over 2M on your hard disk, so you'll probably want to do this once you're certain everything is running correctly.

To delete the setup files:

1. Go to File Manager.

2. Select the \WORDIA directory in the list on the left.

3. Select File Delete from the menu bar.

4. In the Delete dialog box, click OK.

5. In the Confirm Directory Delete dialog box, click Yes.

6. In the Confirm File Delete dialog box, click Yes to All. File Manager will remove all of the Setup files.

In this lesson, you learned where to find Internet Assistant and how to install it. In the next lesson, I'll walk you through the new features and tools that Internet Assistant provides for you.

Lesson

A Quick Tour of Internet Assistant

In this lesson, I'll give you a tour of Internet Assistant and the new features that it gives you.

Looking at the Changes to Word

After you install Internet Assistant, you'll notice a few minor changes to Word. First, there's a new entry called Browse Web in the File menu, as shown in Figure 5.1.

Figure 5.1 You now have a Browse Web command.

Secondly, you have a new icon in the Formatting toolbar, as shown in Figure 5.2.

Note the new icon.

Figure 5.2   You can now click the Web Browser icon to switch to the Web Browse view.

Selecting the File Browse Web command (or clicking the Web Browser icon) will switch Word into Web Browse view and load a convenient starting-points document for you, as shown in Figure 5.3.

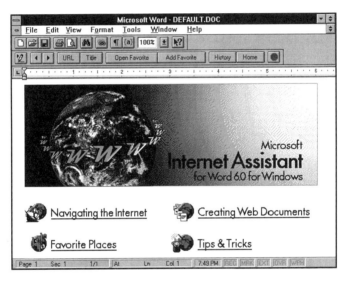

Figure 5.3   The Web Browse view main screen.

Understanding the Internet Assistant Menus

When you're in Web Browse view, you'll notice a whole new set of menus, as shown in the following figures.

Figure 5.4 The File menu.

Here's an explanation of each of the Internet Assistant commands on the File menu:

Command	Explanation
Open URL	Displays a dialog box that lets you type in an URL by hand. Type in the URL, click OK, and Word will download the Web page, format it, and display it on your screen.
Reload	Reloads the current document to reflect any changes that may have occurred.
Close All Web Documents	Each Web document you view is kept in memory as a separate document. Choose this item when you finish browsing to close all of your Web documents. This item will not close any of your regular Word documents.
HTML Document Info	Displays technical information about the current Web document. This is for advanced users of HTML and will not be discussed in this book.

The Edit menu (shown in Figure 5.5) contains commands that you are already familiar with, such as Copy and Paste. The only command on this menu that's unique to Internet Assistant is Copy HyperLink. This command copies the selected hypertext information to the Clipboard. You can then paste this information into a regular Word document.

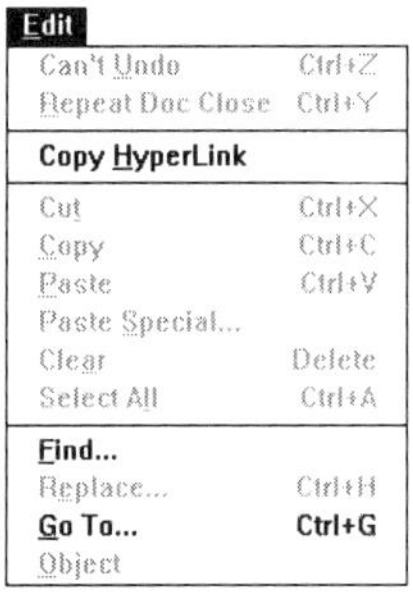

```
Edit
Can't Undo          Ctrl+Z
Repeat Doc Close    Ctrl+Y

Copy HyperLink

Cut                 Ctrl+X
Copy                Ctrl+C
Paste               Ctrl+V
Paste Special...
Clear               Delete
Select All          Ctrl+A

Find...
Replace...          Ctrl+H
Go To...            Ctrl+G
Object
```

Figure 5.5   The Edit menu.

Likewise, the View menu (shown in Figure 5.6) has only two commands that are specific to Internet Assistant. The HTML Edit command switches you to HTML Editor view. The Load Images command is set to [on] by default. If you don't want Internet Assistant to load images, set this to [off] by clicking on the command. Internet Assistant will run much faster with this option set to [off].

```
View
• Normal
  Outline
  Page Layout

  HTML Edit
  Full Screen
  Load Images [on]

  Toolbars...
√ Ruler
  Header and Footer

  Zoom...
```

Figure 5.6   The View menu.

The Tools menu (shown in Figure 5.7) gives you access to Internet Assistant's Favorite Places feature. The Open Favorite Places command loads and displays a list of your favorite Web documents. By choosing the Add To Favorite Places command, you can add the current document to your list of favorite places. For more information on Favorite Places and other features of Internet Assistant, see Lesson 9.

Figure 5.7   The Tools menu.

The commands on the Window menu (shown in Figure 5.8) mainly help you navigate through Web documents you've opened, as described in the following list.

Figure 5.8   The Window menu.

Command	Explanation
Go Back	Reloads the previous document.
Go Forward	Reloads the next document. This option is only valid after Go Back has been used.
Home	Reloads the home page.
History List	Loads and displays a list of all the documents you've seen since you last opened Word.

The Help menu (shown in Figure 5.9) has a couple of commands you may find useful while working with Internet Assistant. Clicking the Internet Assistant for Word Help command displays a Help file with information specific to Internet Assistant. The About Internet Assistant for Word command displays a dialog box with copyright and version number information. (See Lesson 20 for more information on the Help file.)

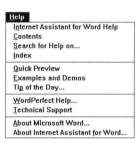

Figure 5.9 The Help menu.

Understanding the Internet Assistant Toolbars

Whenever you are in Web Browse view, you see the Standard and Formatting toolbars. These toolbars give you access to most of the features of Internet Assistant, as described in Table 5.1.

Table 5.1 Internet Assistant Icons

Icon	Description
🔍	Find
🔗	Copy HyperLink
{a}	HTML Hidden
📝	Switch to Edit View

Icon	Description
◀	Go Back
▶	Go Forward
URL	Enter URL Manually
Title	Enter Document Title
Open Favorite	Open Favorites Document
Add Favorite	Add Current URL to Favorites Document
History	Open History List
Home	Switch to Home Page
●	Cancel Download

Understanding Home Pages

Most Web sites contain some sort of home page or starting document. This page links you to most of the documents on the system. In most cases, you'll be presented with the home page if you don't specify a specific document. For example, I could browse to http://www.socketis.net/homepage.html or I could set the Web server to display homepage.html by default and browse to http://www.socketis.net. This makes it easier for you to start.

You should also have a personal home page or starting place that takes you to many different places on the Web. Here are a few good examples (be sure to use uppercased letters as indicated):

- The EINet Galaxy: http://galaxy.einet.net

- Virtual Tourist: http://wings.buffalo.edu/world

- Yahoo: http://akebono.stanford.edu

- World Wide Web Servers: http://info.cern.ch/
  hypertext/DataSources/WWW/Servers.html

Microsoft also provides a good starting-points document that loads when you select Browse Web from the File menu.

This lesson gave you a tour of Internet Assistant and the new menu and toolbar options. In the next lesson, you'll start surfing the Internet.

Lesson

Locating Documents on the Web

In this lesson, you'll learn how to locate documents on the Web. You'll also learn about some of the tools available to you on the Web.

Understanding the Uniform Resource Locator (URL)

Most Web browsers have the capacity to locate Web documents, FTP site directories, and Gopher menus. Internet Assistant is no exception. For this reason, you need to have some sort of universal framework for specifying a resource: the URL (Uniform Resource Locator). You use the URL to locate information resources on the Web.

The URL is divided into three parts:

* **Protocol:** Each type of resource on the Internet uses a different protocol (computer language) for exchanging data between remote hosts and local systems. Therefore, you must tell the Web browser which language it needs to speak before it can do anything; that's why the protocol is the first part of the URL.

* **Domain name:** The second part of the URL tells the Web browser which computer to contact for the information.

- **Path and file name:** After the Web browser has contacted the computer, it asks for whatever it reads in the last part of the URL: a specific file.

  Let's take a closer look at a hypothetical URL and break it down into its parts:

  http://www.que.com/books/10min_guides/ MS_IntAssist.html

  In this example, http (HyperText Transport Protocol) refers to the language you use to transfer the document from the remote host to the local system. The colon (:) separates this field from the rest of the URL.

  The two slashes (//) indicate that a computer name follows. If the file were on your local hard disk, you would see a triple slash instead.

  The next section identifies the name of the computer, in this case, www.que.com. Most computer names are three separate words, each separated by a period. This example indicates the **WWW** server at the **Que com**mercial Internet location. Some computer names, however, can be two words, and some are four or more. The last section (which begins with the first single slash) indicates the path and file name of the Web document.

  Organizing the location process in this manner greatly reduces the time it takes to locate a document. You can browse through a set of documents that are scattered all over the world, yet linked together as if they were on one system.

  Most modern Web browsers do a very good job of keeping the URL hidden from the user so the nontechnical users can use the Internet with greater ease. Most users configure a starting-points document and start clicking from there, completely eliminating the need to understand the URL. However, if you come across a reference to a new document, it's helpful to understand how the URL works. It can also help you search the Internet for more information.

A basic knowledge of the URL is also important when developing a Web site on the Internet. If your documents are going to point to other documents on the Web, you'll want to know how to reference the other documents.

In most cases, however, you'll begin at some starting point and browse, or search for specific information. The next few sections explain some common search engines that Web users use to locate resources on the Internet.

Search Engine   A computer program that searches methodically through a collection of information.

Using EINet Galaxy

EINet is a commercial Internet service provider. It provides Internet access to private and corporate Internet users. As a service to its customers and to the general Internet community, EINet has started the EINet Galaxy home page.

The EINet Galaxy is one of my favorite places to start because it serves as a starting-points document that links to thousands of subject-related documents. EINet also contains a powerful search engine.

To find the EINet Galaxy, follow these steps:

1. Start up Word.

2. Open the File menu and choose Browse Web. Word switches into Web Browse view and loads a convenient starting-points document for you.

3. Click the URL button in the Formatting toolbar. The URL dialog box opens.

4. Type the following URL in the text box and click OK.

      http://galaxy.einet.net

Use Your Favorites Document   To avoid having to type this URL in each time you want to browse the EINet Galaxy, it is a good idea to add this URL to your Favorites Document. I'll explain how to do this in Lesson 9.

Internet Assistant takes you to the EINet Galaxy home page, as shown in Figure 6.1.

Figure 6.1   The EINet Galaxy home page.

Using the EINet Galaxy as a starting-points document is quite simple. The first section of the document contains several paragraphs filled with hypertext links, which appear as blue underlined words, to other documents. All you have to do is click a link that looks interesting.

Most of the links off the main Galaxy page are references to other documents on the Galaxy. EINet maintains a rather extensive collection of Galaxy pages that users can browse to find information. The EINet Galaxy pages each contain a command menu with the following options that you can use to navigate the features and information in the EINet Galaxy:

Up   Takes you to the previous level. Like most Web sites, information is organized in a hierarchical structure to make it easier to locate. However, I would recommend that you use the left arrow button on the toolbar to go back. This button will load a document in the cache from disk instead of reloading the document from the Internet (which takes much longer).

Home   Takes you to the main EINet Galaxy page. This has no effect if you're already at the main page, of course.

Help   Takes you to the Help page (with a very cool graphic of the moon!). This page gives step-by-step instructions for accessing and searching for information at the EINet Galaxy and the rest of the World Wide Web.

Search   Takes you to a comprehensive (but not complete) list of Web search engines. Which one should you use? That's a difficult question to answer; try a few of them and stick with the one that you find easiest to use.

EINet Galaxy   Takes you to a page containing information about the EINet Galaxy. Most of this information is useful only if you're curious about EINet.

If you move to the bottom of the main EINet page, you'll notice a section where you can initiate a search (see Figure 6.2). This section is an example of a search engine. It's quite handy because it can search the EINet Galaxy pages as well as the rest of the Web. In addition, it can also locate Gopher menus that match your search. (I will explain the Gopher menu system in Lesson 8.)

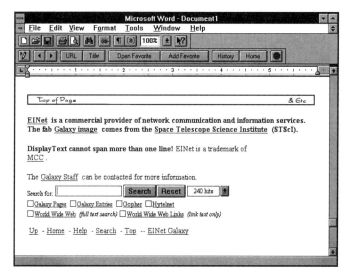

Figure 6.2 The EINet Galaxy search engine.

The EINet search engine is very easy to use. Here are the steps to follow:

1. Go to the bottom of the main page (or any other Galaxy page).

2. In the box labeled Search for: type a word that relates to the topic you want information on. For example, if you're looking for information on fish, type fish.

3. Click the Search button. After a few seconds (or minutes, sometimes), you see a list of related pages.

Each related page is listed as a hypertext link to that page. Click each one to see the actual page.

I Don't See Anything Useful!   If you don't
see any useful information in the pages that it
gives you, you might want to refine your search.
For example, if you typed **fish** the first time, you
can try **trout** or **carp** or something else more specific.
This process can take a few moments for the beginning
user. Don't worry, you'll get the hang of it.

By default, the search engine will search through
Galaxy pages and Galaxy entries (I'll explain these terms in
the next section). You can also limit the scope of the search
by selecting the type of information you want the search
engine to search for. You'll notice several check boxes
underneath the search form (where you typed the word
fish):

Galaxy Pages   Returns only pages in the Galaxy
itself. This helps you find collections of references to
related information.

Galaxy Entries   Returns only the titles of information references in the Galaxy pages. This helps you
find a very specific information reference.

Gopher   Returns titles of Gopher menus. I will
explain Gopher in Lesson 8.

Hytelnet   Returns pages of the hypertext telnet
database. Since Internet Assistant does not support
telnet, I recommend that you do not use the Hytelnet
search.

World Wide Web Text   Searches the text of the
thousands of Web pages referenced in the Galaxy.

World Wide Web Links   Searches the links found in the World Wide Web text searches. This returns more specific information than World Wide Web Text.

Using WebCrawler

The WebCrawler is another tool for searching the Web; it uses a search method called a *depth-first search*. It starts with a set of documents and visits each link in each document, building an index of all the URLs and the topics to which they relate. However, it also follows some guidelines to keep it from utilizing too many Internet resources or bogging down a specific computer.

Each search engine on the WebCrawler computer is limited to one document per minute on any given computer. This cuts down on the amount of traffic it generates on each computer. The engines are also limited to a certain number of documents per day from each computer. Since it runs constantly, it is still quite capable of keeping up.

As the WebCrawler performs each search, it saves the results of the search. This way, each subsequent user can tap into the "knowledge base" of the WebCrawler. If I search for "textiles" and get a list of Web pages, and then you search for "textiles" two minutes later, it will give you the same list instead of searching the whole Internet again.

This accumulative knowledge is extremely valuable and has made the WebCrawler a very popular place for searches. Current estimates rate the WebCrawler at over 2,000,000 users per month.

To access the WebCrawler, follow these steps:

1. From Word's Web Browsing mode, click the URL button in the Formatting toolbar. The URL dialog box opens.

2. Type the following URL in the text box and click OK.

> **http://webcrawler.cs.washington.edu**

You should see the page shown in Figure 6.3.

Click here to go to the search page.

Figure 6.3   The WebCrawler home page.

At this point, you can read a bit about the WebCrawler, or you can choose the WebCrawler Search Page link at the end of the first paragraph. This link will take you to the WebCrawler search page shown in Figure 6.4, which you can use to search for information resources.

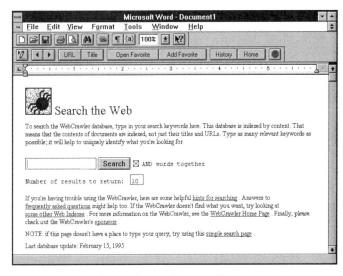

Figure 6.4 The WebCrawler search page.

To use the WebCrawler search page:

1. Type your keyword (such as **fish**) in the blank area.

2. Click the Search button.

As with the EINet search engine, you'll see a list of hypertext links to documents that relate to your topic. You may have to refine or reword your search to get the information you're looking for. Take your time and be patient. You'll get the hang of it after a few tries.

Using the World Wide Web Worm

Usually referred to as WWWW, the World Wide Web Worm is quite similar in scope and execution to the WebCrawler. WWWW is quite popular among the Internet community because of its complex searching algorithms.

To access the World Wide Web Worm, follow these steps:

1. From Word's Web Browsing mode, click the URL button in the Formatting toolbar. The URL dialog box opens.

2. Type in the following URL in the text box and click OK.

> http://www.cs.colorado.edu/home/
> mcbryan/WWWW.html

You see the home page shown in Figure 6.5.

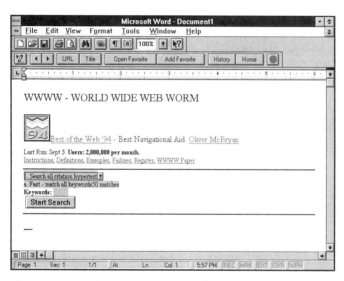

Figure 6.5   The World Wide Web Worm.

To start searching for documents, you must first select the kind of search you want to do from the Select drop-down list. WWWW allows you to perform any of the following types of searches:

- Search all citation hypertext
- Search all citation addresses
- Search only in HTML titles
- Search only in HTML addresses

The trick to using WWWW effectively is learning which search method to use. I'll give you some basic examples that should clear things up for you.

Before I begin, I should explain a few terms. The author of the World Wide Web Worm uses different terminology from what I use here. To keep you from getting too confused, let me explain each one; then I'll give an example of how to use them.

Search all citation hypertext Citation hypertext is the same thing as an anchor or a hypertext link. Citation hypertext refers to the little underlined words that point to other documents. This type will search the actual underlined words you would see on your screen.

Search all citation addresses Citation address refers to the URL that a hyperlink points to (confusing, huh?). This type will search the actual URL of the hypertext link. This is handy for searching for information based on location or a particular computer.

Search only in HTML titles Each HTML document has its own title. This type will search the text of the title of the document.

Search only in HTML addresses This type will also search the actual URL of a document. So what's the difference between this one and Search all citation addresses? **Search all citation addresses** searches the URLs in the hyperlink of a document, while **Search only in HTML addresses** searches the URL of the actual document.

This Is So Confusing! If these explanations only confuse you more, use the following examples to determine the type of search you need to use. This search engine is very powerful—and with power comes complication.

If you want to search for all the Web pages about fruit, use search type #3: **Search only in HTML titles** and search for **fruit**. Theoretically, any document about fruit would probably have fruit in the title.

If you want to search for all the Web pages from Washington University in St. Louis, use search type #2: **Search only in HTML addresses** and search for **wustl**. Any document found on the Washington University computer system would have wustl in the title. How do I know that? After months of experience on the Web, you'll begin to remember the abbreviations of the popular Web sites on the Internet.

If you want to search for all the Web pages that have hypertext links to documents about the Simpsons TV show, use search type #1: **Search all citation hypertext** and search for **Simpsons**.

If you want to search for all the JPEG (a type of graphics compression used extensively on the Internet) graphics files referenced by other documents, use search type #4: **Search only in HTML addresses** and search for **jpg**. Any JPEG image will have a file extension of .jpg.

To perform a search with the World Wide Web Worm:

1. Type your keywords in the blank area. Keywords are the information topic you're looking for, such as fruit, Simpsons, wustl, or jpg.

2. Set the search type based on the type of information you're looking for. If you're not sure, use search type #1: Search all citation hypertext.

3. Click the Search button.

After a few moments, the World Wide Web Worm will send you a list of hypertext links to documents related to the keywords you've typed in. You may need to refine or reword your search to get the result you need. Don't worry, you'll get the hang of it.

For more information about WWWW, browse the other links available from the WWWW home page. The Introduction is especially interesting.

More Search Engines   If you're looking for a list of good search engines, browse to either of these URLs:

http://www.yahoo.com/Reference/ Searching_the_Web

http://www.iquest.net/iq/reference.html

In this lesson, you learned how to locate documents on the Web. You also learned how to use EINet Galaxy, WebCrawler, and the World Wide Web Worm to find materials on the Web. In the next lesson, you'll learn about transferring files from remote systems with FTP.

Lesson

Using FTP with Internet Assistant

In this lesson, you'll learn about FTP and how to use it with Internet Assistant. You'll also learn how to understand UNIX directory listings so you can find the information you want.

Understanding FTP

FTP stands for *file transfer protocol*. It has one simple job: transferring files. In order to better understand how FTP works with Internet Assistant, you need some background information.

FTP is a popular UNIX utility that has become widely used over the Internet. Many versions of FTP programs have been written for many different operating systems. Most Windows FTP programs look and act a lot like File Manager. Essentially, they provide a list of local and remote files and buttons that copy files to and from the remote system.

Internet Assistant also provides support for FTP. However, instead of the file windows, you see a list of files and directories that look like a DOS directory.

Connecting to an FTP Site

FTP sites also require an URL. Although the URL looks a little bit different from a Web URL, it still maintains the same basic form. Here's a sample URL for the FTP site at Microsoft:

ftp://ftp.microsoft.com/deskapps

This URL specifies the FTP protocol, the machine name (ftp.microsoft.com), and the directory to list (/deskapps).

If you enter this URL into Internet Assistant, you'll see a directory listing like the one shown in Figure 7.1.

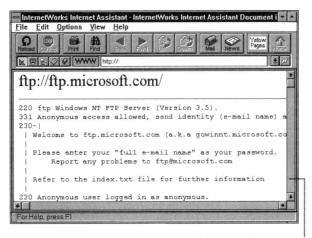

Use the scroll bar to view files.

Figure 7.1 An FTP directory listing.

To connect to an FTP site, follow these steps:

1. In Word, open the File menu and select the Browse Web command.

2. Click the URL button in the toolbar. The Open URL dialog box appears.

3. In the text box, type **ftp://**.

4. Type the domain name of the machine and then type a forward slash (/).

5. Type in the full path to the file you want to download, and then type a forward slash (/).

6. If you know it, type in the name of the file you want
to download (otherwise, just click OK and Internet
Assistant will give you a list of all the files in that
directory). If you type in the exact file name,
Internet Assistant immediately starts downloading
the file when you click OK.

Moving Through the Directories

Most computers on the Internet do not run MS-DOS or
Microsoft Windows; they run UNIX. This can be a disadvan-
tage to some Internet users since they won't be very familiar
with the UNIX file system. The biggest obstacle for most
beginning Internet users is the UNIX directory listings from
FTP sites.

In most cases, you need to be able to figure out three
things from a UNIX directory listing:

- Is the entry a file or directory?

- If the entry is a file, how large is it?

- What is the name of the file or directory?

If you can get these three pieces of information from
the following UNIX directory entry, then you'll be fine in the
FTP world.

Take a look at Figure 7.2. The first field contains a list of
rights or *permissions*. The only character that you'll need to
concern yourself with is the first one. If the first character is
a dash, the listing is for a file. You can download this file, if
you want. If the character is a letter **d**, the listing is for a
directory. The other characters refer to read, write, and
execute permissions on the file system. For the most part,
though, if you can see it in the list, you can download it.

Permissions   Group   Date   File/directory name

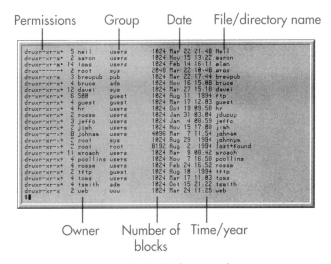

Owner   Number of   Time/year
blocks

Figure 7.2 A sample UNIX directory listing.

The second and third fields contain information about the owner (creator) of the file and the group to which that user belongs. Don't worry about these unless you have an account on the system. If you have an account on the system, you can access certain areas of the computer, but not others. These areas will be determined by the ownership and the permissions list in the first section. Most FTP users use anonymous FTP and have access only to a very limited section of a computer. In this case, the ownership of the file is not very important at all.

The next few sections of the directory listing give information about the size of the file and the time and date of last modification. The final field contains the actual name of the file or directory.

Internet Assistant makes changing directories very simple. If you want to change to a specific directory, click its name in the directory listing. Internet Assistant will automatically send a command to the remote host to change to that directory. Afterwards, it will automatically update the directory listing for the new directory.

Downloading Files

Internet Assistant also makes the task of downloading files simple and painless. To download a file, click its name in the directory listing. Internet Assistant automatically sends a command to the remote system to send the file you requested.

Let's walk through a sample FTP download. This example will download the Internet Assistant Readme file from the Microsoft FTP Service.

1. Start Word (if you've haven't already).

2. Open the File menu and select Browse Web. You see the default Internet Assistant Web document.

3. Click the URL button in the Formatting toolbar. You see the Open URL dialog box.

4. Type ftp://ftp.microsoft.com in the Enter URL field and click OK. Internet Assistant downloads the file listing from the FTP server at Microsoft. (Figure 7.1 shows the screen you should see.)

5. Use the scroll bar on the right to scroll down the page. You should begin to see a list of files in green underlined text. Figure 7.3 shows a sample file listing (this may be different from what you see).

6. Click on peropsys to open that directory. You'll find it on the right side of the file listing. Internet Assistant displays a list of the files in the peropsys directory (see Figure 7.4).

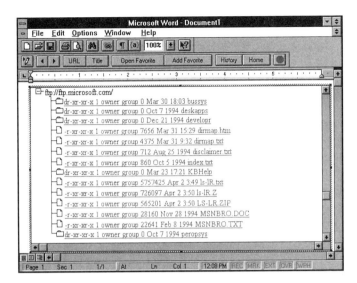

Figure 7.3 The Microsoft file listing.

Open directory

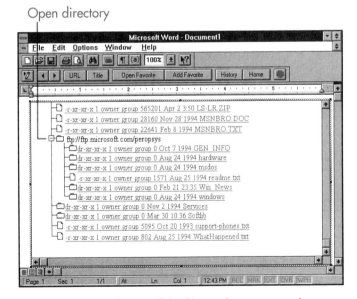

Figure 7.4 A listing of the files in the peropsys directory.

7. Click on readme.txt. You'll find it on the right side of the file listing. Internet Assistant retrieves the file and displays it on-screen (see Figure 7.5). Use the scroll bar to get back to the beginning of the document.

8. Click the right mouse button to view a menu of your options, as shown in Figure 7.5. Choose Save As to display the Save As dialog box.

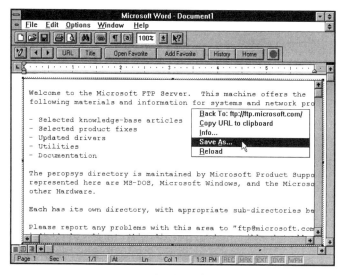

Figure 7.5 On-screen display of readme.txt with right mouse button menu.

9. Use the Save As dialog box to indicate the path and file name you want to use to save this file. Click OK when you finish.

If you click a binary file, you will see the message shown in Figure 7.6 instead of the actual file, but you can click the right mouse button and choose the Save As command to save the file.

Binary File   A file that is usually a program or a compressed data file. Binary files can't be read or understood by people.

Plain English

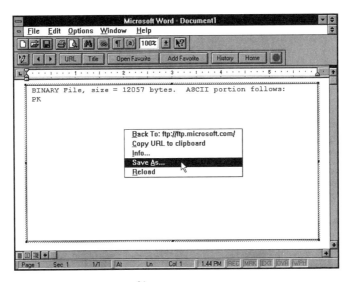

Figure 7.6   Binary file message.

After you've downloaded the file, you can use the URL button to type in a new URL or consult your Favorites document to continue browsing the Web.

In this lesson, you learned about FTP, how UNIX directories work, and how to download files off the Internet with Internet Assistant's FTP support. In the next lesson, you'll learn about Gopher, how Gopher menus work, and how to browse gopherspace with Internet Assistant.

Lesson

Using Gopher with Internet Assistant

In this lesson, you'll learn about Gopher, how it works, and how to use it with Internet Assistant.

Understanding Gopher

Gopher was developed at the University of Minnesota. It may be no surprise to you that the gopher is their mascot. However, the gopher has another relevance: you dig around like a gopher for information at Gopher sites (called *gopherspace*).

> **Gopherspace** A large collection of menus that point to other menus and text files. You can browse through these menus and text files to gopher to (find) all kinds of information.

The Internet community often refers to Gopher as a first-generation browsing utility. It actually works in much the same way as the World Wide Web, but does not have the attractive graphical display.

Gopher differs from the Web; it's menu-based while the Web is based on documents. The hypertext functionality is still present, though. With Gopher, each menu item points to either another menu of choices, or to a text file containing some kind of information. Gopher menus can point to resources on the same computer or another computer on the network.

Connecting to Gopher Sites

Internet Assistant, like most Web browsers, uses the URL to access Gopher sites. The URL looks a little bit like the one we used for FTP and the World Wide Web. Here's a sample URL for the University of Missouri Gopher server:

gopher://showme.missouri.edu/global/ref/ internet/docu/history

This URL specifies the Gopher protocol, the domain name (showme.missouri.edu), and the directory to list (/global/ref/internet/docu/history).

If you were to enter this URL into Internet Assistant, you would see a Gopher menu similar to Figure 8.1.

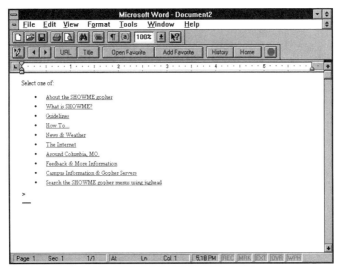

Figure 8.1 A Gopher menu in Internet Assistant.

To connect to a Gopher site, use the following formula to create the URL:

1. Type gopher://.

2. Type the domain name of the machine.

3. Type a forward slash (/).

4. Type in the full path to the menu you want to view.

5. Type a forward slash (/).

Moving Through the Menus

Internet Assistant makes Gopher simple to use. Each menu appears on the screen in a clear fashion. To explore a menu on the next level, click the choice in the menu on your screen. Internet Assistant automatically sends a command to the remote system, downloads the next menu, and displays it on your screen.

The easiest way to understand Gopher is to become familiar with using it. Let's walk through a sample Gopher session:

1. Start Word (if you've haven't already).

2. Open the File menu and select the Browse Web command. You see the default Internet Assistant Web document.

3. Click the URL button in the Formatting toolbar. You see the Open URL dialog box.

4. Type gopher://gopher.micro.umn.edu in the Enter URL field and click OK. Internet Assistant will download the Gopher menu from the Gopher server at the University of Minnesota. Figure 8.2 shows the screen you should see.

5. Click Fun & Games. You should see the Fun & Games menu as shown in Figure 8.3.

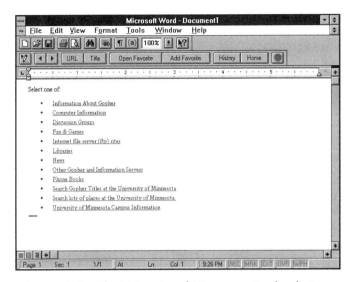

Figure 8.2 The University of Minnesota Gopher listing.

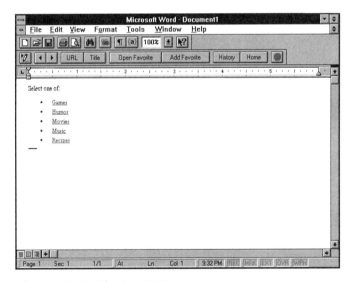

Figure 8.3 The Fun & Games menu.

6. Select Humor. You see the Humor menu in Figure 8.4.

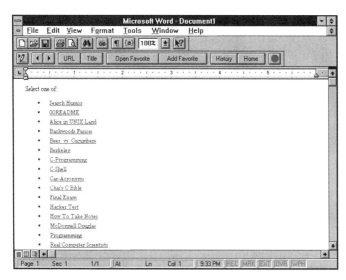

Figure 8.4   The Humor menu.

7. Select Alice in UNIX Land. Internet Assistant will retrieve the file and display it on the screen for you (see Figure 8.5).

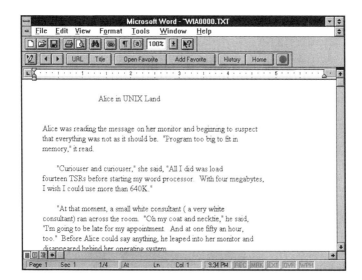

Figure 8.5   Alice in UNIX Land document.

At this point, the document exists as a temporary file (usually called **~WIA0000.TXT**). If you want to save the document as a Word document:

1. Open the File menu and select the Save As command. You see the Save As dialog box.

2. Select Word Document from the Save File As Type drop-down list box at the bottom.

3. Type a name for the file in the File Name edit field.

4. Click OK.

You can now edit the document as a normal Word document.

In this lesson, you learned about Gopher, how it works, and how to use it with Internet Assistant. In the next lesson, you'll learn how Internet Assistant keeps track of Web pages you've already viewed. You'll also learn how to get back to your favorite Web pages.

Lesson

Retracing Your Steps

In this lesson, you'll learn how Internet Assistant keeps track of Web pages you've already viewed. You'll also learn how to get back to your favorite Web pages.

Redisplaying Pages from the Document Cache

If you browse the Web often, you'll soon find yourself in this situation: you've just downloaded a page that you didn't want to see, and you want to go back to the previous page. If the current page doesn't have a link back to the previous page, you'll have to start all over again from the home page. This can be quite time-consuming.

Fortunately, Internet Assistant uses a *document cache* (pronounced "cash"), which is essentially a temporary directory. During each Web browsing session, Internet Assistant saves each document you open and the graphics that go along with it to a document cache.

You use the arrows on the toolbar in Web Browse view to navigate through the document cache:

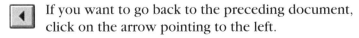 If you want to go back to the preceding document, click on the arrow pointing to the left.

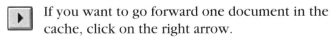 If you want to go forward one document in the cache, click on the right arrow.

The document cache will be erased whenever Word is shut down. However, there are other tools available that will keep track of documents permanently on the hard disk.

Reloading Documents from the History List

As you continue to become more familiar with the Internet, you'll find yourself saying, "You know, I'd really like to take another look at that one document I saw a couple weeks ago." Well, Internet Assistant has a solution for you: the history list.

Internet Assistant keeps track of the last 50 Web documents you have opened during your Web browsing sessions. It stores the locations (URLs) of each of these documents in a file called the history list. You can consult this list at any point in time to reload a document. Unlike the document cache, the history list is not erased when you shut down Word. However, only the URL is stored in the history list.

If you've already viewed a few Web documents, you should be able to see a few items in this list. To check, click on the History button in the Formatting toolbar in Web Browse view. You can also choose the History List command from the Window menu while you're in Web Browse view. Figure 9.1 shows an example of a history list window.

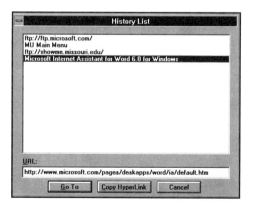

Figure 9.1 A history list.

When you select an item from the history list, Word downloads the document again from the remote site.

Deleting URLs from the History List

Sometimes, you may browse to a Web page you don't want saved in your history list. (This may limit the number of useful entries in the history list.) If you are familiar with Windows .INI files, you can remove an item from the history list by modifying a file called HTMLHIST.INI. To delete an entry from the history list, follow these steps:

.INI File A small text file that contains initialization information for a program. It can also contain personalized settings for the program or interface.

Plain
English

1. To switch to Program Manager, press Ctrl+Esc and double-click Program Manager.

2. Open the File menu and select Run. The Run dialog box appears.

3. In the Command Line box, type htmlhist.ini, and then click the OK button. A Notepad window appears with the .INI file loaded.

4. In the [History] section, delete the entries you want to remove from the history list.

5. In the [URL] section, delete the lines that correspond to the entries you deleted in the previous step. The number at the end of the entry in the [URL] section indicates the number of the entry in the [History] section.

6. Open the File menu and select Exit. A dialog box appears asking you to confirm your changes.

7. Choose Yes from the dialog box.

8. Exit Word.

When you start Word again, the items you've removed will no longer appear in the history list.

Saving URLs in the Favorite Places Document

Over the past couple of years, Web browsers have added features to increase productivity of WWW users. Perhaps the most popular feature is the *bookmark list*, or list of favorite Web pages. Internet Assistant calls this list the Favorite Places Document.

The Favorite Places Document is a collection of URLs that point to your favorite Web pages on the Internet. When you first install Internet Assistant, there is one entry that will show you some cool places to help you start.

To view the Favorite Places Document, click on the Open Favorite button in the Formatting toolbar in Web Browse view. Or open the View menu and choose the Favorites Document command while you are in Web Browse view. Figure 9.2 shows a sample Favorite Places Document.

You can add items to this list of favorites as you find Web pages that you may want to visit again in the future. To add an URL to the Favorite Places Document, browse to the document you want to add and then click on the Add Favorite button in the Formatting toolbar. There is no limit (other than hard disk space) to the number of entries in your Favorite Places Document.

Figure 9.2   The default Favorite Places Document.

To go back to a document in your Favorite Places Document, click the Favorite button on the Formatting toolbar. After the Favorite Places Document loads, double-click on the name of the document you want to see.

In this lesson, you learned about the ways Internet Assistant helps you keep track of Web documents on the Internet. In the next lesson, you'll learn the basics of creating your own Web documents with Internet Assistant.

Lesson

Designing Web Pages

In this lesson, you'll learn the basics of designing effective Web pages.

If you plan to design Web pages, chances are you'll want someone else to look at them. I'll also make another bet: If you're taking the time to design and produce Web pages, and you want someone to look at them, you're probably trying to make money (or at least increase the amount of money you're already making) by setting up a Web site on the Internet to serve your customers better. In this case, appearance is very important.

The term browse does a good job of describing how people work with the World Wide Web. Web users quickly look through documents they come across until they find something that interests them. Your document must get your point across quickly and efficiently, or the user will move on to another page. A Web page cluttered with fonts and pictures will prevent readers from quickly understanding your message. This lesson explains some general concepts to remember when designing your Web pages.

Using Text Formatting

Most Web pages have a design similar to the layout of these lessons. They start out with a Title. Then, there is a Main Heading, or Level 1 Heading. Under each heading is normal text. In some cases, there are subheadings, or Level 2 Headings.

Writing good HTML documents (like any other craft) takes time and practice. First, let me give you a general list of conventions to follow:

- Use headers and normal text in most cases. Don't get too carried away with fancy formatting; it only confuses the reader of your document. Lesson 19 shows you how to use different styles to change the appearance of your text.

- Try to make the document read smoothly. The best advice: Write the document first, and then make hyperlinks out of some of the text.

- Avoid the use of "click here to…." Instead, provide a meaningful word or phrase to use a hyperlink. For example:

  Good: We also have a text-only version of this page.

  Bad: Click here to see a text-only version of this page.

  Lesson 12 shows you how to create a hypertext link to another document.

- Whenever possible, include bulleted lists of topics or additional resources. For example:

  You can find more information on the following topics:

  - Price structure
  - Names and addresses of our distributors
  - A complete online catalog of ABC's products

  This is easy to understand. Lesson 14 shows you how to create a bulleted list.

- Use horizontal rules to separate main sections of a document. Also, any time you would normally use a page break (force a new page), use a horizontal rule. Lesson 14 shows you how to create a horizontal rule.

Figures 10.1 and 10.2 show examples of bad formatting and good formatting.

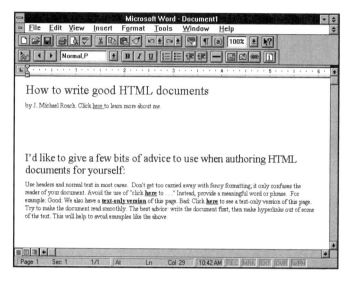

Figure 10.1   Bad HTML formatting.

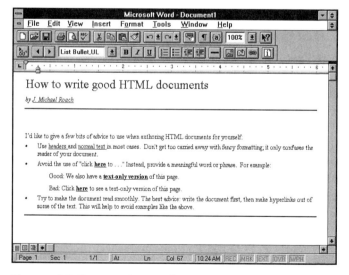

Figure 10.2   Good HTML formatting.

Notice how I use italics instead of large fonts to offset some important information. I also carefully lay out lists to illustrate my point and use hard rules to separate sections. If I have more information on a topic, I simply make the related word a hyperlink.

Using Graphics

One of the most powerful features of the World Wide Web today is the ability to include pictures and graphics in documents. The most important rule to follow when using graphics is this: don't use too many pictures and graphics. The temptation to do so is strong, but there are several reasons for avoiding the use of pictures and graphics except where necessary:

- Pictures and graphics take a lot of time to download.

- If pictures and graphics are too big, the user can't see any text on the screen (see Figure 10.3).

- If there are too many pictures and graphics, the user will have to wait a long time before he can read your document (see Figure 10.4).

- If the pictures and graphics are necessary to understand the document, users without graphical Web browsers won't be able to understand your documents (this is becoming less of an issue as graphical Web browsers become more prominent).

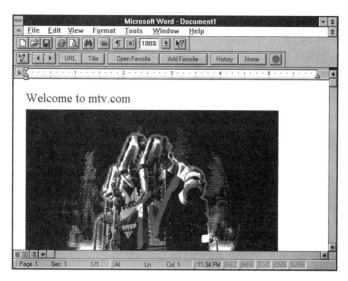

Figure 10.3   This graphic is too big.

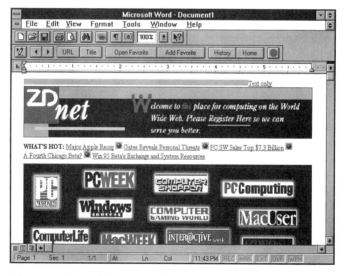

Figure 10.4   Too many pictures.

Figure 10.5 shows a Web page that uses graphics well. This graphic is an *inline graphic*. You learn how to insert inline graphics in Lesson 13.

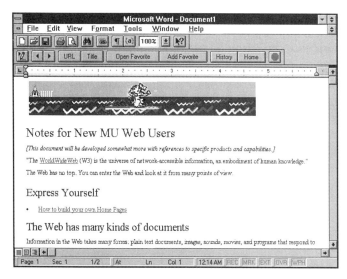

Figure 10.5   This inline graphic adds interest to the Web page without distracting you from the text.

In this lesson, you learned the basics of designing a document for the Web. In the next lesson, you'll learn to use Internet Assistant to create HTML documents.

Lesson

Writing HTML Documents with Word

In this lesson, you'll learn the basics of writing HTML documents with Internet Assistant for Word.

Creating an HTML Document

There are three ways to create an HTML document. You can start with an existing Web document, you can start with an existing Word document (see Lesson 17), or you can start from scratch.

To create an HTML document from an existing Web document, follow these steps:

1. From Word, open the File menu and choose the Browse Web command. Internet Assistant's Web Browse view opens.

2. Navigate to the Web document that you want to use as the basis for your HTML document.

 3. Click the HTML Edit button in the toolbar to switch to HTML Edit view. From this view, you can add and format text as covered in the next section.

If you want to create an HTML document from scratch, follow these steps:

1. Open the File menu and select New. You see the New dialog box.

2. Select HTML in the list of Templates.

3. Click OK to exit the New dialog box. You will be in HTML Edit view.

Formatting Your HTML Document

In Lesson 10, you learned about the importance of good design in creating effective Web pages. Internet Assistant provides you with several easy-to-use tools that will help you create great-looking Web pages. To use these tools, you first must be in HTML Edit view. You can switch to this view by opening the View menu and choosing HTML Edit or clicking the HTML Edit icon (it looks like a pencil) in Web Browse view. The following sections explain how to use styles and the Formatting toolbar to enhance the look of your HTML document.

Using Styles

When you're in HTML Edit view, you can see that the Formatting toolbar contains the familiar Style drop-down list box. In this list, you see a complete listing of HTML styles, including normal paragraph text, the various levels of headings, bulleted and numbered lists, and many others.

To use styles to format your document, follow these steps:

1. Open your document in HTML Edit view. If you're starting your document from scratch, enter your text as you would in any Word document.

2. Select the text you want to apply the style to.

3. Click the arrow next to Style drop-down list to display the list of available styles. Click the one you want. Internet Assistant applies the style to the selected text.

Unlike other Word templates, you can't add or modify the styles on the HTML template or your HTML document might not work correctly.

Using the Formatting Toolbar

To format your HTML document with the Formatting toolbar, follow these steps:

1. Open your HTML document in HTML Edit view.

2. Select the text you want to change.

3. Click the appropriate button in the toolbar.

Table 11.1 explains what the buttons in the Formatting toolbar do.

Table 11.1 Formatting Toolbar Buttons

Button	Description
B	Makes the selected text bold.
I	Adds italics to the selected text.
U	Underlines the selected text.
⅛	Changes the selected text into a numbered list (same as List Number style).
⅛	Changes the selected text into a bulleted list (same as List Bullet style).
彗	Decreases the indent in the selected text.
彗	Increases the indent in the selected text.

In this lesson, you learned the basics of creating HTML documents with Internet Assistant. In the next lesson, you'll learn how to create links to other HTML documents.

Lesson

Inserting a Hypertext Link

In this lesson, you'll learn how to create a hypertext link to another Web document in your HTML documents.

Using Hypertext and Hyperlinks

Most people who create Web documents want to link their documents to other documents on the Web using a technology called *hypertext*.

> **Hypertext** A technology that links network resources together. Each resource contains hyperlinks to other resources.

Each hypertext link (also called a *hyperlink*) "points to" another document and tells the Web browser to load that document and display it on the screen. This new document will usually contain hyperlinks, as well.

Hypertext uses two distinct types of links: *specific* and *relative*. Although technically it makes no difference which one you use, choosing the correct type can make your life much easier if you need to make changes to a document later on. The next two sections explain each of the types and give you guidance on which to use.

Creating a Specific Link

A *specific link* specifies the entire URL of a Web document. You usually use a specific link when you want to create a link to an Internet resource on a different computer.

Specific links can point to any kind of resource on the Internet, such as:

- HTML documents
- FTP directories
- Gopher menus
- Sound or animation files

Remember that the user's Web browser must support the type of resource you're pointing to for the link to work correctly. Although Internet Assistant is not full-featured as a Web browser (it only supports HTML, FTP, and Gopher), most browsers will support the types listed above. To avoid any confusion for your user, be sure to explain in the document that contains the links any reference to resources other than HTML, FTP, and Gopher. Notify the user that his Web browser must support the technology.

In addition, you can create links with graphics instead of text. I'll explain how to use graphics and pictures as links in Lesson 13.

To specify a word or phrase as a specific link:

1. Open the document you want to add a link to in HTML Edit view.

2. Highlight the word or phrase you want to be a link.

3. Click the HyperLink button in the Formatting toolbar. The HyperLink <A> dialog box appears on-screen, as shown in Figure 12.1.

Type your
URL in the
blank or
select from
the list.

Click to
create the
hyperlink.

Figure 12.1   Creating a hyperlink.

4. Click the to URL tab in the dialog box.

5. Type the entire URL in or select one from the list of URLs you've used in the past. Internet Assistant conveniently saves them for you.

6. Click OK to close the HyperLink <A> dialog box and create the hyperlink.

Using Relative Links

A *relative link* is a link that points to a resource relative to the current URL. For example, if you were to include a link to an inline graphic in your document, and that graphic were in the same directory as your HTML document, you could specify just the file name for the graphic instead of the entire URL. The Web browser would assume the same computer and directory.

It's important to remember that the only difference between a relative and specific link is the amount of information in the link. The advantage of a relative link is that if you were to move the document and graphic to another location, you wouldn't need to update the link in the document with the new location of the graphic. Furthermore, if you use relative links, you can move an entire set of documents to another directory—or even another computer—without having to update any of the links.

In most cases, relative links will refer to inline graphics for your documents or other documents on your Web site. For the most part, use specific links only to specify Internet resources on another computer. Otherwise, use relative links.

Creating a Link to a Local Document

Internet Assistant supports the following types of local documents (or image files on your computer):

- Word documents (.DOC)

- HTML documents stored in ASCII text (.HTM)

- Write documents (.WRI)

- ASCII text files (.TXT)

- Bitmapped images (.BMP)

  To specify a link to a local resource:

1. Open the document you want to add a link to in HTML Edit view.

2. Highlight the word or phrase you want to be a link.

 3. Click the HyperLink button in the Formatting toolbar. The HyperLink <A> dialog box appears on-screen, as shown in Figure 12.2.

Figure 12.2   The HyperLink <A> dialog box.

4. Click the to Local Document tab in the dialog box.

5. Use the directory tree on the right to specify the directory in which the document resides.

6. Type in the file name or select the name of the file in the list on the left.

7. Click OK.

Creating a Link to a Bookmark

Bookmarks provide a quick way to jump to a specific part of a long document. Links to bookmarks are most often used in very long HTML documents that contain several sections. Each section is bookmarked and links to those bookmarks are included at the beginning of a document.

HTML bookmarks work in much the same way as Word document bookmarks. If you use bookmarks in Word, you'll appreciate this because the interface is the same; you won't have to learn anything new about creating bookmarks in your HTML documents.

Of course, you must create a bookmark in your document before you can create a link to that bookmark. To create a bookmark in your HTML document:

1. Open your document in HTML Edit view.

2. Place your cursor where you want the bookmark to be.

3. Open the Edit menu and select Bookmark. The Bookmark dialog box opens.

4. Type a name for your bookmark (use something descriptive) in the Bookmark Name text box.

5. Click the Add button.

Once you've created a bookmark, you can reference that bookmark with a hypertext link. To insert a hypertext link to a bookmark:

1. Open the document you want to add a link to in HTML Edit view.

2. Select the word or phrase you want to link to your bookmark.

3. Open the Insert menu and select HyperLink. You see the HyperLink <A> dialog box, as shown in Figure 12.3.

4. Click the to Bookmark tab.

5. Select the bookmark you want to link to in the list of available bookmarks.

6. Click OK.

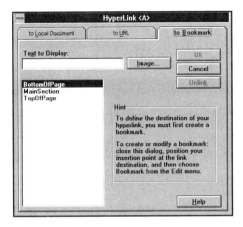

Figure 12.3   Inserting a hypertext link to a bookmark.

In this lesson, you learned how to create specific and relative hypertext links to Internet resources in your HTML documents. In the next lesson, you'll learn how to insert pictures and graphics into your documents.

Lesson

Using Graphics in HTML Documents

In this lesson, you'll learn how to insert pictures and graphics into your HTML documents. You'll also learn how to use pictures and graphics as links to other resources.

Using Inline Graphics

Any picture or graphic included in a document is an *inline graphic*. Figure 13.1 shows an example of how you can use an inline graphic on your Web page.

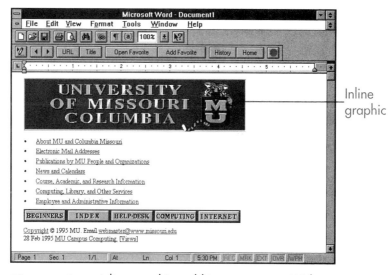

Figure 13.1   Inline graphics add interest to your Web pages.

Here are a few other examples of how you can use inline graphics:

- Include a .GIF of your company logo in your Home Page.

- Include a small .GIF of your face in a personal Home Page.

- Use .GIFs as icons in front of headers or as bullets in a list.

- Use small, decorative .GIFs to enhance the appearance of your document.

Choosing the Right Type of Graphic

For the most part, pictures and graphics used in HTML documents need to be in CompuServe Graphics Interchange Format (.GIF format). Most of the newer Web browsers also support inline JPEG (.JPG) graphics, as well. The choice is yours, but you need to choose one of these two. It's possible to include graphics in other formats, but most of the time you won't be able to use them as inline graphics. You'll have to create a link to them. Lesson 12 shows you how to create a hyperlink.

Whenever possible, keep your inline graphics files smaller than 10,000 bytes. I know that's not very much, but it makes a big difference when someone is downloading your document over a 9600 baud modem. Yes, 9600 baud is still very popular for using the Internet over a modem.

It's also a good idea to use as few colors as possible when creating the graphic. For example, most icons and decorative graphic work can be done in 16 colors. Photographs, however, typically require 256-color resolution. Although every .GIF is saved as a 256-color graphic, reducing the number of colors cuts down on decode time and reduces the overall size of the file, as well.

Inserting Inline Graphics into Your HTML Documents

Internet Assistant gives you convenient point-and-click access to insert pictures and graphics into your Web documents. To insert a picture or graphic into a Web document, follow these steps:

1. Open the document in HTML Edit view.

2. Place your cursor where you want the picture or graphic to be.

3. Open the Insert menu and select the Picture command. The Insert Picture dialog appears, as shown in Figure 13.2.

Insert Picture   You can also use the Picture button in the Formatting toolbar.

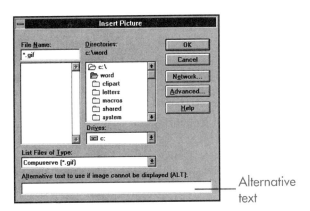

Alternative text

Figure 13.2   The Insert Picture dialog box.

4. Use the Directories box to specify the location of your picture or graphic.

5. Select either .GIF or .JPG (based on the format of your picture or graphic) under List Files of Type.

6. Type the name of the file under File Name or select it from the list.

7. Type in an alternative word or phrase (for browsers that do not display graphics) under Alternative text to use if image cannot be displayed. This text will only appear if the browser will not display graphics.

8. Click OK to close the dialog and insert the picture or graphic.

Using Graphics as Links to Other Resources

Another powerful feature of HTML is the ability to use graphics as links to other resources. The most popular application for this feature is creating icons for hypertext links. Many HTML pages will contain lists of other documents and resources with an icon next to each one. The icon is linked to the same resource as the hypertext. Figure 13.3 shows an example of icons being used in this way.

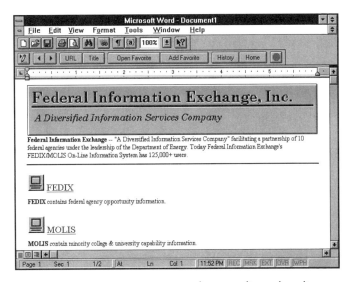

Figure 13.3   Using icons to enhance a list or heading.

Creating a Link to a Local Document

Using pictures and graphics as links to other documents is as simple as creating any other kind of link. To create a graphical link to a local document:

1. Open the View menu and select HTML Edit.

2. Place your cursor where you want the link to be in your document.

3. Open the Insert menu and select the HyperLink command. The Hyperlink dialog box appears.

4. Click the to Local Document tab.

5. Click the Image button. You see the Insert Picture dialog box.

6. Use the directory tree on the right to specify the location of the graphic you want to use.

7. Select .GIF or .JPG from the Files of Type drop-down list box.

8. Type the file name or select it from the list.

9. Click OK to close the Insert Picture Dialog box.

10. Use the directory tree to specify the location of the local resource.

11. Type the file name or select it from the list.

12. Click OK to close the Hyperlink dialog box.

Creating a Link to an Internet Resource

To create a graphical link to an Internet Resource (URL):

1. Place your cursor where you want the link to be in your document.

2. Open the Insert menu and select HyperLink. The Hyperlink dialog box appears.

3. Click the to URL tab.

4. Click the Image button. The Insert Picture dialog box appears.

5. Use the directory tree on the right to specify the location of the graphic.

6. Select .GIF or .JPG from the List Files of Type drop-down list box.

7. Type the graphic's file name in the File Name text box, or select it from the list.

8. In the text box at the bottom of the dialog box, type the text to be displayed if a Web browser cannot show graphics.

9. Click OK to close the Insert Picture dialog box.

10. Type the URL in the text box, or select a previously used URL from the list.

11. Click OK.

Creating a Link to a Bookmark

To create a graphical link to a bookmark within the same document:

1. Place your cursor where you want the link to be in your document.

2. Open the Insert menu and select HyperLink. The Hyperlink dialog box appears.

3. Click the to Bookmark tab. You see the Insert Picture dialog box.

4. Click the Image button.

5. Use the directory tree on the right to specify the location of the graphic.

6. Select .GIF or .JPG from the List Files of Type drop-down list box.

7. Click OK. You are back at the Hyperlink dialog box.

8. Highlight the bookmark you want to create a link for.

9. Click OK to insert the hyperlink and close the dialog box.

In this lesson, you learned how to insert pictures and graphics into your HTML documents. You also learned how to use pictures and graphics as links to other resources. In the next lesson, you'll learn how to insert horizontal rules into your document and use graphics as icons and list bullets.

Lesson

Creating Horizontal Rules and Icons

In this lesson, you'll learn how to insert horizontal rules into your document, use graphics as icons for bulleted lists, and create icons for headers.

Creating Horizontal Rules

Creating simple, yet attractive, documents is the key to the success of your Web site. The simplest way to enhance the appearance of your HTML document is to use horizontal rules, as demonstrated in Figure 14.1.

Horizontal Rule A thick black horizontal line that separates sections of a document.

With Internet Assistant, inserting a horizontal rule into a document is easy. Here are the steps to follow:

1. Open your HTML document in HTML Edit view.

2. Place your cursor where you want the horizontal rule to appear.

3. Select Horizontal Rule from the Style drop-down list box.

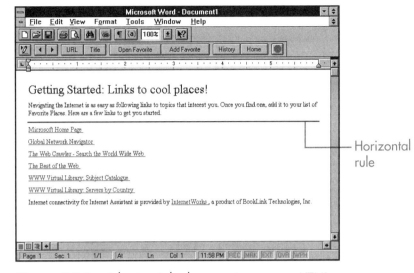

Horizontal rule

Figure 14.1   A horizontal rule can spice up your HTML documents.

Quick Horizontal Rules   Instead of choosing Horizontal Rule from the Style drop-down list box, you can just click the Horizontal Rule button in the Formatting toolbar.

Horizontal rules can be a great tool for jazzing up the appearance of your document, but sometimes you'll want to do more than add little black lines everywhere. You can also create long, thin graphical designs, save them as .GIFs, and include them as an inline image instead of using a horizontal rule. To review this process, see Lesson 13.

.GIF (Graphics Interchange Format)   A graphics file format commonly used in Web documents.

Using Graphics as Icons for Lists and Headers

Another way to greatly enhance the look of your document is to create small graphics (about the size of a Windows icon) and use them in headers and lists. Take a look at Figure 14.2.

.GIF graphic as list bullet

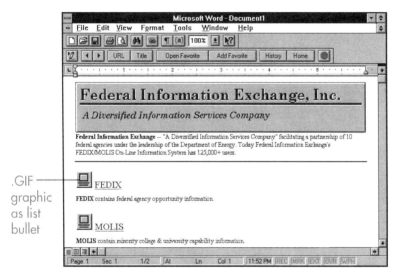

Figure 14.2   Icons used in lists.

Using icons in lists and headers can do wonders for an otherwise drab document. Let's take a closer look at each technique.

Creating Custom Bulleted Lists

Be creative with graphics and icons in your document. Although Internet Assistant (and other Web browsers) automatically use a special round character for bulleted lists, you can also create your own small "ball-looking" characters in various colors and save them as .GIFs. You can then use these characters as inline graphics for creating your own custom bullets for lists. Don't use the List Bullet style, however. Instead, create each bullet manually. Follow these steps:

1. In HTML edit view, type out each entry in the list (be sure to press Enter after each one).

2. Place your cursor at the beginning of the first item.

3. Open the Insert menu and select the Picture command. The Insert Picture dialog box appears.

4. Choose GIF or JPG from the List Files of Type dropdown list box.

5. Use the directory tree on the right to indicate the location of your bullet graphic.

6. Type the file name, or select it from the list on the left.

7. Click OK.

Your first item should now contain a bullet. Repeat steps 2–7 for each item in your list. This can take quite a bit of time, but the end results are worth it; normal lists appear boring after a while, and a good-looking list will attract attention.

Creating Icons for Headers

You can be just as creative with graphics and icons in your document headers. These icons can help to set your document apart from the rest the documents on your Web site, giving each page a unique look. To create icons for headers, use the same basic process as for creating icons for custom bulleted lists:

1. In HTML edit view, type out the header.

2. Change the text to a Header style using the dropdown list in the Formatting toolbar.

3. Place your cursor at the beginning of the header.

4. Open the Insert menu and select the Picture command. The Insert Picture dialog box appears.

5. Choose GIF or JPG from the List Files of Type drop-down list box.

> **More Icons** You can find a lot of .GIF icons at http://akebono.stanford.edu/yahoo /Computers/World_Wide_Web/Programming/ Icons/.

6. Use the directory tree on the right to indicate the location of your bullet graphic.

7. Type the file name, or select it from the list on the left.

8. Click OK.

> **Two-Way Hyperlinks** Most people these days use an icon and text for a header and link the icon and the text to the same document.

In this lesson, you learned how to use horizontal rules and small graphics to liven up the look of your documents. In the next lesson, you'll learn how to create fill-out forms to use in your Web documents.

Lesson

Creating a Fill-Out Form

In this lesson, you'll learn about fill-out forms and how you can use them to allow users to interact with your Web presence.

Creating a Form

In most cases, a form is used to get some sort of information from the user—for example, signing onto the Web server (to keep track of users who see your Web pages) or registering a product (such as software).

Some companies have been quite creative with fill-out forms. Pizza Hut now maintains a site (http://www.pizzahut.com) that allows a user to order pizza over the Internet. Sorry, this service is only available in a limited area, but you can still get a demo of how it works.

Most forms work in a simple manner. The Web document contains code that tells the Web browser to insert text boxes, check boxes, and drop-down list boxes in the document. These elements are *form fields*. The user types text into a text box, checks or unchecks a check box, and selects an item from a drop-down list box. Figure 15.1 illustrates the various types of form fields.

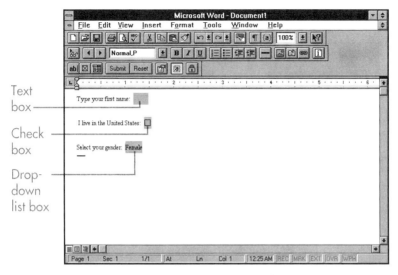

Text box

Check box

Drop-down list box

Figure 15.1   The different types of form fields.

After the user has filled out the form, he clicks on the Submit button. This causes Internet Assistant (or any other browser) to send the form data to a remote system. The remote system has a program running on it that looks for incoming forms and processes them.

Internet Assistant uses Word's Form command capabilities to create HTML forms. With the Internet Assistant Forms toolbar, you can create simple forms to submit information and to perform Web searches. To create a blank form in your Web document:

1. In HTML Edit view, type all of your document, so you'll know where your form field is going to be in relation to the entire document.

2. Place your cursor where you want your form field to be.

3. Open the Insert menu and select the Form Field command. A message will appear reminding you that you are creating a new form.

4. Click Continue. Two boundaries will appear in your document: Top Of Form and Bottom Of Form. The Forms toolbar will also appear, as will the Form Field dialog box.

> **This Is Different Than Word!**   In Internet
> Assistant, you use the Insert Form Field command
> to create an entire HTML form. The Insert Form
> Field command behaves differently in Word,
> where it inserts a single form field at a time.

5. Click the Cancel button on the Form Field dialog box to close it.

You should now have a blank and empty form area. At this point, you may begin to create a layout for the form itself. Type in any text that will appear in the form. For example, type **Enter your name:**. After all the text is in place, you should see your form as you want it to appear.

Adding Form Fields

To add form fields, such as check boxes, to your blank form, follow these steps:

1. For each field (Name, Address, or whatever), place your cursor where your want the user to type in the information (or check a box, or select an option).

2. Click the button on the Forms toolbar that corresponds to the type of form field you want to put in that place.

Table 15.1 explains what each of the form fields does and shows the corresponding tools in the Forms toolbar.

Table 15.1 Form Field Tools

Button	Form Field Name	When to Use It
[ab]	Text box	Use it any time you want the user to type information such as a name or address.
[⊠]	Check box	Use it any time you want the user to indicate Yes or No to a question. For example, if your form is used to register a piece of software, you can use a check box to ask the customer: Have you used a previous version of our software?
[▤]	Drop-down list box	Use it any time a question will have a certain number of answers, and the user can simply choose one. For example, "How did you hear about our product?" For this question, you could create a list box with Friend, Relative, Co-worker, Advertisement, and Salesperson in it.

From time to time, you may need to update your entire form or change the appearance of a form field. Each form field has its own set of options. However, not all of the options apply to Internet Assistant (remember, Internet Assistant uses Word's built-in form support). To change the options or appearance of a form field, double-click the form field in the document. A dialog box relating to that type of form field appears, as shown in the following figures.

Form Field Options You can also click the form field in your document, and then click the Form Field Options button in the Forms toolbar to change the options or appearance of a form field.

Figure 15.2 shows the Text Form Field Options dialog box. The text form field has only one option that relates to Internet Assistant. You can change the default text (under Default Text) that appears in the text field (normally this is left blank, however). The rest of the options do not apply to Internet Assistant. Click OK to save your changes and close the dialog box.

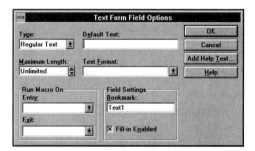

Figure 15.2 The Text Form Field Options dialog box.

Figure 15.3 shows the Check Box Form Field Options dialog box. The check box form field has only one option that relates to Internet Assistant. You can change the default value (checked or not checked) of the check box. The rest of the options do not apply to Internet Assistant. Click OK to save your changes and close the dialog box.

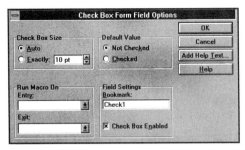

Figure 15.3   The Check Box Form Field Options dialog box.

Figure 15.4 shows the Drop-Down Form Field Options dialog box. The drop-down form field has several options that can be changed, but again, only a few of them are used by Internet Assistant.

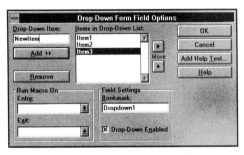

Figure 15.4   The Drop-Down Form Field Options dialog box.

- In the Drop-Down Item field, type each item (one at a time) and click Add >>. The new item appears in the Items in Drop-Down List field.

- If you want to remove an item from the list, highlight the item in the Items in Drop-Down List field, and click Remove. The item will disappear from the list.

- If you want to change the order of the items in the list, highlight the item that is out of order and use the up arrow and down arrow buttons to the right of the Items in Drop-Down List field.

* Click OK to save your changes and close the dialog box.

Putting the Finishing Touches on Your Form

After you add all the form fields to your form, follow these steps to complete your form:

1. To give the user a way to submit the form for processing, put your cursor where you want to insert a Submit button, and click the Submit button in the Forms toolbar.

2. In the Form Submit Button dialog box that appears, type the submission information at the bottom of the dialog box. In order for your form to function properly and send the form data correctly, you need to identify your remote system properly. Without this information, the Web browser has no idea how to submit the form. If this information is unclear to you, read the "Making Your Forms Work" section in this lesson.

3. You can choose the text that will appear on the Submit button by selecting the Text radio button and typing the text in the edit field to the right of the Text radio button. If you'd like the Submit button to contain a picture or graphic instead, select the Custom Button radio button, and click Select Picture. From here, follow the procedure described in Lesson 13. Click the OK button when you finish. Internet Assistant adds the Submit button to your form.

4. To enable a user to restore all form-field values back to their defaults after filling out and submitting the form, you must provide a Reset button. Place your cursor where you want the Reset button to appear, and click the Reset button from the Forms toolbar. Internet Assistant adds a Reset button to your form.

5. To visually differentiate the form from the rest of the document, insert a horizontal rule before and after the form. See Lesson 14 for instructions on how to do this.

 6. When you finish creating your form, click the Protect Form on the Forms toolbar.

Making Your Forms Work

Although Internet Assistant contains the necessary tools to create forms, it does not contain any features for actually using forms. It is important to realize that forms must be handled by external programs (called CGI programs) written to receive the incoming data and act upon it.

CGI (Common Gateway Interface)
A specification for external programs (such as Web browsers) to interact with servers (such as Web servers).

To fully implement your forms on a Web server, you must have your system administrator set up these programs. If you are the system administrator (or just interested) and you are not familiar with how forms work with the World Wide Web, browse to the following URL:

http://www.ncsa.uiuc.edu/SDG/Software /Mosaic/Docs/fill-out-forms/overview.html

This link contains vast resources to answer almost all your questions about implementing form support for your Web site.

In this lesson, you learned how to use Internet Assistant to create fill-out forms for your Web documents. In the next lessons, you'll learn to how to use existing HTML documents to create your own HTML documents and how to convert existing HTML documents into Word.

Using an Existing HTML Document

In this lesson, you'll learn how to convert existing HTML documents to Word format or how to use them to create your own HTML documents.

Using Web Documents in Word

Internet Assistant gives you the ability to copy information from the Internet and paste it into your own Word documents. This feature makes compiling reports and other tasks much simpler and easier.

With other Web browsers, it is possible to copy the text from a document. However, you can't usually copy the graphics, which are sometimes very important to the content of the document. Also, in most cases, only the text is copied, not the formatting. This means that headers and lists will have to be reformatted once you copy them into your document.

Internet Assistant does not have any of these limitations. Because Internet Assistant converts the document as it downloads it, you can copy information from any HTML or Web document into a Word document.

Follow these steps:

1. In Word, open the document that you want to copy Web information into.

2. Open the File menu and select the Browse Web command. Internet Assistant starts and opens Web Browse view.

3. Click the URL button in the Formatting toolbar.

4. Type the URL of the Web document that contains the text you want to copy in the Open URL text box. Internet Assistant opens the document.

5. Select the part of the document that you want to copy. You can include text and graphics.

6. Open the Edit menu and choose Copy.

7. Open the Window menu and choose your Word document to switch back to Word.

8. Position the insertion point in the document where you want the Web information to be copied, and then open the Edit menu and choose Paste. The Web information is now part of your Word document.

Converting from HTML to Word Format

You'll also want to be able to save documents you find on the Web. In most cases, you'll save them as Word documents. This gives you the ability to change them, edit them, add tables, or whatever else you'd like to do. To convert a Web document to a Word document:

1. In Word, open the File menu and select Browse Web. Web Browse view opens.

2. Download the document you want to convert by browsing to it or using the URL button on the toolbar.

3. Open the File menu and select the Save As command. The Save As dialog box appears.

4. Type a name for the file in the File Name: box.

5. Choose Word Document from the Save File as Type drop-down list box.

6. Click OK. Your document now resides on your hard disk as a Word document.

Switching Back to the Normal Template

If you're familiar with Word, you'll recall that, by default, most documents are produced using the Normal template. If you convert your HTML documents to Word format, you'll notice that they use the HTML template instead. This can present a number of problems for users who are familiar with using the Normal template:

- The styles in the Normal template will not be available.

- The toolbars (and any changes you've made) will not be available.

- Any other changes made to the Normal template will not be reflected in your newly converted document.

Fortunately, the process of changing back to the Normal template is quite simple. This method simply attaches a different template to the existing document, but still uses the HTML template styles:

1. Retrieve (or open) the HTML document you want to convert.

2. Open the View menu and select HTML Edit. HTML Edit view opens.

3. Open the File menu and select Templates. You should see the Templates and Add-ins dialog box.

4. Click Attach. You should see the Attach Template dialog box.

5. In the list on the left, highlight Normal.DOT.

6. Click OK. This takes you back to the Templates and Add-ins dialog box.

7. Click OK. The template you selected should now be attached to your document.

Using HTML Documents in Your Own HTML Document

Perhaps the single most popular use for Internet Assistant is the ability to use existing HTML documents to create your own documents. This idea may have occurred to you before. You're surfing the Internet and you come across a beautifully designed Web page. You say to yourself, "Wow, would I like to have something like that in *my* Web page!" Internet Assistant makes that possible.

With Internet Assistant, copying from one HTML document to another couldn't be simpler. Follow these steps:

1. In Word, open the File menu and select Browse Web. You switch to Web Browse view.

2. Download the document you want to copy by browsing to it or using the URL button on the toolbar.

3. Open the View menu and select HTML Edit.

4. Using your mouse, highlight the section you want to copy.

5. Open the Edit menu and select Copy. This copies the selected text (including formatting data) to the Windows Clipboard.

6. Open the File menu and select New. You should see a blank document before you.

7. Open the Edit menu and select Paste.

You can repeat the copy/paste process as many times as you like to get information (including hyperlinks!) from other documents.

Viewing the Markup of an HTML Document

At some point, you're probably going to want to see the actual HTML code of your document. For example, you may want to modify hyperlinks in your document using the Replace command. To do this, you must first display the HTML code for hyperlinks; then you can use the Find and Replace commands as you would with regular Word text.

Fortunately, Internet Assistant prevents the need to view HTML code very often. However, if you want to view your HTML code, there are two ways to do it.

 To view the hidden HTML code in your document for Word fields, click the HTML Hidden button in the Standard toolbar.

> **It's Not All Here!** Remember, the HTML Hidden button only displays HTML code for Word fields. This includes form fields and hyperlinks, but does not include the HTML code for paragraphs, headings, and the rest. To view the entire code, you must view your document as an ASCII text file.

To view your document in straight ASCII text and HTML code:

1. Open the File menu and select Save As.

2. Select HTML from Save File as Type in the Save As dialog box.

3. Click OK.

4. Open the File menu and select Close.

5. Open the File menu and select Open. The Open dialog box appears.

6. Check the Confirm Conversion check box.

7. Highlight the name of the HTML document you want to view.

8. Click OK. The Confirm Conversion dialog box appears.

9. Select Text Only from the Convert File From list.

10. Click OK.

You should see your document as ASCII text and HTML markup code. This document can be edited (if, for example, you want to include HTML code that Internet Assistant does not support) and resaved as an ASCII text file.

In this lesson, you learned how to use existing HTML documents to create your own, or how to convert them to Word format. In the next lesson, you'll learn how to convert existing Word documents to HTML for use on the Internet.

Lesson

Converting Word Documents to HTML

In this lesson, you'll learn how to create HTML documents from existing Word documents.

What HTML Formatting Does Word Support?

HTML is changing every day. Although Internet Assistant does not support the up-and-coming HTML 3.0 specification, it does have support for the basic HTML functions. In order to get your document as close as possible to what you want, it is important to understand which formatting features are available in HTML and which are not.

Let's go over the basic Word styles and formatting features available in HTML:

- Normal paragraph style

- Bulleted lists

- Numbered lists

- Headings (available in seven layers, Heading 1 through Heading 7)

- Embedded graphics (although not those embedded via the Clipboard; you must embed them from a file)

- Form fields (for creating fill-out forms)

These are the basic HTML formatting features available, and for the most part, these are the only ones you'll use. However, there are some more advanced HTML formatting features that Word does not support:

- Line justifications (centering and so on)
- Formatted tables
- Backgrounds

If you know how to use the above formatting features, you can still use them. Refer back to Lesson 16 to view the markup of your document and edit the HTML code by hand. I use this method quite often and find that even though Internet Assistant does not support all of the HTML code I'd like to use, I can still put the bulk of a document together in about 25 percent of the time it would normally take. At that point, I put the last touches on the document by hand with a text editor.

What Is Lost When You Convert to HTML?

Although HTML is a powerful and flexible language, it does not have support for all of the formatting features available in Microsoft Word. Therefore, Internet Assistant does not convert these formatting features when you convert your Word document to HTML. Even when you create a document using Internet Assistant, some elements may not be preserved because they are not valid HTML. As Internet Assistant saves your document, it simply ignores invalid HTML markup that your document might produce.

Word elements that are not converted to HTML include:

- Annotations
- Automatic numbering of lines and headings
- Borders and shading

- Captions
- Character formatting (fonts and emphasis)
- Drawing layer elements
- Fields (only the field result is converted)
- Footnotes and endnotes
- Frames
- Graphics embedded via the Clipboard
- Graphics included in Pre or Blockquote paragraphs
- Headers and footers
- Indented paragraphs in any paragraph style other than OL or UL
- Index entries
- OLE objects
- Page breaks and section breaks
- Revision marks
- Tabs in any paragraph style other than Pre and DL
- Table of Contents entries

Redesigning Your Document for HTML

Since the stylistic features listed above will not be included in your HTML document, it is important to get a good idea of what your document will look like without them. There are two ways to do this. You can remove the formatting and features listed above from your Word document, or you can load the Word document, save it as HTML, and then re-open the HTML document. Anything not converted, of course, will not appear.

The second method is much easier to use, of course. Remember, however, to select HTML in the Save File as Type drop-down list box in the Save As dialog box. When I create a new HTML document, I use this method so I can be as certain as possible as to the final appearance of my document. Remember, each Web browser displays your document differently. With a little experience and bit of experimentation, you'll begin to create great-looking HTML document with very little effort.

You can try this process with any existing Word document—it's actually kind of fun. It's especially fun if you have a copy of Netscape or Mosaic to view your final document with. Let's walk through one quickly:

1. Open any existing Word document (preferably one that's not very long).

2. After your document is finished loading, open the File menu and select the Save As command. The Save As dialog box opens.

3. Select HyperText Markup Language from the Save File as Type drop-down list box.

4. Open the File menu and select Close. Don't worry, your original document is still intact.

5. Open the File menu and select Open. The Open dialog box appears.

6. Select HyperText Markup Language from the List Files of Type drop-down list box.

7. Highlight the name of your document in the list under File Name.

8. Click OK. You should see the saved version of your HTML document.

If you notice anything different about your document from when you saved it, those formatting features are not supported by Internet Assistant.

In this lesson, you learned how to create HTML documents from existing Word documents. In the next lesson, you'll learn how to use the hyperlink features of Internet Assistant to link Word documents together.

Lesson

Using Hyperlinks in Word Documents

In this lesson, you'll learn how to use the hyperlink features of Internet Assistant to link Word documents to other Word documents, as well as to Internet documents.

Inserting Hyperlinks to Web Pages in Word Documents

Perhaps the coolest thing about Internet Assistant is the ability to create a hyperlink to a Web document in a Word document. You can also create hyperlinks to FTP sites and Gopher menus. Anyone who has Internet Assistant and an Internet connection can open this document and click the hyperlink to get a current version of the Web page.

Internet Assistant makes this task easy. Each time you download a Web document, Word remembers its URL. A simple command will copy that URL to the Clipboard. After that, it's as simple as pasting it into a Word document. Here's how to do it:

1. Open the Word document you want to link to an Internet resource.

2. Switch to Web Browse view by opening the File menu and choosing Browse Web.

3. Browse to the document you want to link to.

4. After the Web document is done downloading, open the Edit menu and select the Copy HyperLink command.

5. Switch back to the Word document by choosing it from the Window menu.

6. Place your cursor where you want the hyperlink to be.

7. Open the Edit menu and select Paste. You should see a blue, underlined copy of the title of Web document in your Word document. This is a hyperlink to that HTML document.

To edit the text that appears in the hyperlink:

1. Highlight the hyperlink.

2. Click the hyperlink with your right mouse button. You should see a small pop-up menu.

3. Click Toggle Field Codes. You should see some extra text.

4. You can edit the text in underlined blue; you can change this text to whatever you like. It's usually best, of course, to give some indication of what document you're linking to. Be careful not to delete or edit the field code itself (if you do, you can use the Undo button in the Standard toolbar to take back the edits).

5. After you complete your edit, click the field with the right mouse button and select Toggle Field Codes once again. The extra text should disappear from your screen.

Creating a Local Web of Word Documents

In addition to the ability to create links to Internet documents, you can also create links to other Word documents on your own local area network. This capability is especially powerful in the corporate environment trying to achieve the "paperless" office. A series of local Word documents linked to one another is a *local Web*.

> **Local Area Network**   A collection of computers (usually in the same building) connected together with some type of wire. The computers on this network all use the same "computer language" to share information.

Local Webs can be useful in a number of different ways. You can be as creative as you like when coming up with ways to use the local Web capabilities of Internet Assistant. One application of this technology that pops into my mind is internal documentation frequently updated and passed around to perhaps hundreds of employees. A good example might be your employee handbook. Instead of creating new versions of the handbook each year and paying for hundreds of copies, you could have the entire documentation online. Well, you can have the documentation online without the use of Internet Assistant, so what's the big advantage? It's simple:

An employee handbook (or any similar document) can be quite large. This presents two major disadvantages:

- The document often will not fit in memory (or if it does, the computer will not run very well).

- The document has to be divided into smaller documents that the user has to load in one at a time.

Internet Assistant will allow you to use the second example (using smaller documents) but instead of the user having to load each document manually (after digging around the network to find it), your main document could be a "Table of Contents" that contains hyperlinks to the various other documents that compose the entire handbook. Each chapter of the handbook can contain links to other pertinent documents as well.

Notice that if you need to update one small detail (maybe you've added a holiday to the list of paid holidays), you can update one line in one document and everyone in the company has a current version—with no incremental printing costs.

Furthermore, if your company consists of more than one office connected via a wide area network, such as the Internet, your entire company could keep resources such as these in one central location. This would also cut down on costs considerably.

Wide Area Network   A network of networks, usually several LANs (local area networks) connected together. The Internet is an example of a wide area network.

Creating a link to another Word document is similar in process to creating a link to an Internet resource.

To create the link:

1. Open the Word document you want to link to another Word document.

2. In Web Browse view, open the Word document you want to link to.

3. Open the Edit menu and select Copy HyperLink.

4. Switch back to the other Word document (you can access it from the Window menu).

5. Place your cursor where you want the hyperlink to be.

6. Open the Edit menu and select Paste. You should see a blue, underlined copy of the title in your Word document. This is a hyperlink to that HTML document.

Once again, you can edit the text that appears in the hyperlink. Follow these steps:

1. Highlight the hyperlink.

2. Click the hyperlink with your right mouse button. You should see a small pop-up menu.

3. Click Toggle Field Codes. You should see some extra text now.

4. You will now be able to edit the text in underlined blue. Be careful not to delete or edit the field code itself (if you do, you can use the Undo button in the Standard toolbar to take back the edits).

5. After you complete your edit, click the field with the right mouse button and select Toggle Field Codes once again. The extra text should disappear from your screen.

You can use these capabilities for hundreds of different reasons—the only limit is your imagination.

Using a Word Document with Hyperlinks

This process of using hyperlinks in Word documents works just like the Web browsing features of Internet Assistant. The user wanting to access the Word documents via a hyperlink must have Internet Assistant installed on his or her PC as well. To use a hyperlink:

1. Open the File menu and select Open. The Open dialog box appears. You see a list of available documents.

2. Highlight a document that contains a hyperlink and click OK.

3. After the document finishes loading, you see a phrase in blue, underlined text. Click that phrase. This should cause another document to open in Word automatically.

In this lesson, you learned how to link your Word documents to HTML documents as well as to other Word documents. In the next lesson, you'll learn how to customize your copy of Internet Assistant to your own tastes.

Lesson

Customizing Internet Assistant

In this lesson, you will learn how to customize your copy of Internet Assistant for your own taste.

Changing the Number of Web Documents That Are Open at the Same Time

By default, Internet Assistant will keep a maximum of 10 Web documents open at the same time during a Web browsing session. This means that as you browse the Web, the last 10 documents you looked at are still loaded in memory. You can change this default. Lowering the default number (I prefer to change it to one or two) saves a lot of memory and improves performance.

To change the number of Web documents Internet Assistant will keep open:

1. Open the File menu and select the Open command. You see the Open dialog box.

2. Highlight your Windows directory in the Directories box.

3. Check the Confirm Conversions option in the lower right corner.

4. In the File Name box, type **wordhtml.ini** and then choose OK.

5. Highlight Text Only in the Convert File From dialog box and click OK. The WORDHTML.INI file opens on-screen.

6. Find the [MISC] section; then find the line that reads **AllowedOpenDocs=10**. If you don't see this line, insert a blank line and type it in as you see it here.

7. Change the **10** to the number of Web documents you want open at the same time.

8. Open the File menu and select the Save command. Select Text Only from the Save File as Type drop-down list.

9. Restart Word.

The changes will take effect the next time you open Word and select Browse Web from the File menu.

Changing the Appearance of Text in Web Browse View

By default, Internet Assistant will use 12-point Times New Roman (larger for headers) to display your Web pages. You may want to change this. For example, I prefer 10-point Arial. If you want to change the defaults, here's how:

1. Load any Web document. Choose one from your list of favorites, if you want.

2. Open the Format menu and select Style. You should see the Style dialog box.

3. Highlight the style you want to modify in the Styles box.

4. Click Modify. You see the Modify Style dialog box, as shown in Figure 19.1.

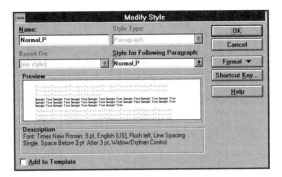

Figure 19.1 The Modify Style dialog box.

5. Click Format. You see a small drop-down menu.

6. Select the style attribute you want to change. You can change the font and size of the text, as well as the alignment of paragraph styles. For example, you could specify that all headers are centered. You can also add a border to a particular style.

7. Check the Add to Template item if you want this change to affect all of your HTML documents.

8. Click OK. This takes you back to the Style dialog box.

9. Click Apply. You return to the open Web document where you can see your newly formatted text.

Changing the Color of Hyperlinks in Web Browse View

By default, Internet Assistant will display hyperlinks in blue. If you want, you can change the color of the hyperlinks by modifying a line in WORDHTML.INI.

To change the color of hyperlinks:

1. Open the File menu and select the Open command. You see the Open dialog box.

2. Highlight your Windows directory in the Directories box.

3. Check the Confirm Conversions entry in the lower right-hand corner.

4. In the File Name box, type **wordhtml.ini** and then choose OK. The Convert File From dialog box appears.

5. Highlight Text Only and click OK. The WORDHTML.INI file opens on-screen.

6. Find the [MISC] section; then find the line that reads **AnchorColor=blue**. If you don't see this line, you can add it to the file as you see it here.

7. Change the word **blue** to the one of the following colors (whichever you like best; feel free to experiment):

Black	DarkCyan
Cyan	DarkGreen
Green	DarkMagenta
Magenta	DarkRed
Red	DarkYellow
Yellow	DarkGray
White	LightGray
Dark Blue	

8. Open the Select File menu and select Save.

9. Restart Word.

The changes will take effect the next time you open Word and choose Browse Web from the File menu.

Changing DEFAULT.DOC

By default, Internet Assistant loads a document called DEFAULT.DOC when you select Web Browse view. Figure 19.2 shows the document.

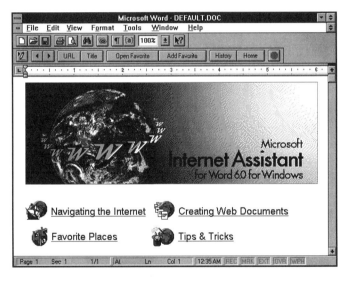

Figure 19.2 DEFAULT.DOC.

You can change this document, create a new one, or specify a different file name to load. To change this document, edit DEFAULT.DOC as you would any other HTML document. You can include links to Web pages or other local documents.

To create a new one, rename DEFAULT.DOC (unless you're sure you don't want to keep it), create a new document (include hyperlinks to your favorite starting points), and save it as DEFAULT.DOC. Save this file in the same directory as the original DEFAULT.DOC (now renamed). Usually, this directory is C:\WINWORD\INTERNET.

To specify a different document to load, follow these steps:

1. Open the File menu and select Open. You see the Open dialog box.

2. Highlight your Windows directory in the Directories box.

3. Check the Confirm Conversions option in the lower right-hand corner.

4. In the File Name box, type **wordhtml.ini** and then choose OK. The Convert File From dialog box appears.

5. Highlight Text Only in the Convert File From dialog box and click OK. The WORDHTML.INI file opens on-screen.

6. Find the [MISC] section; then find the line that reads **StartDoc=C:\WINWORD\INTERNET\DEFAULT.DOC**. The path shown may not match your document; this is the default.

7. Change **C:\WINWORD\INTERNET\DEFAULT.DOC** to the full path and file name of the document you want to load when you open the File menu and select the Browse Web command.

8. Open the File menu and select Save.

9. Restart Word.

The changes will take effect the next time you open Word and choose Browse Web from the File menu.

Changing the Length of the History List

As you've learned, Internet Assistant automatically keeps track of all the pages you've viewed during the current session. By default, Internet Assistant will also save the last 50 URLs you've browsed to a history file. However, you can change the number of URLs stored in the history list by modifying HTMLHIST.INI. Lesson 9 explains the history list in more detail.

To change the length of the history list:

1. Open the File menu and select Open. You see the Open dialog box.

2. Highlight your Windows directory in the Directories box.

3. Check the Confirm Conversions entry in the lower right-hand corner.

4. In the File Name box, type **htmlHIST.ini** and then choose OK. The Convert File From dialog box appears.

5. Highlight Text Only in the Convert File From dialog box and click OK. The **HTMLHIST.INI** file opens on-screen.

6. Find the [Config] section; then find the line that reads **MRULength=50**. If you don't see this line, you can add it to the file as you see it here.

7. Change the **50** to any number except **0**.

8. Open the File menu and select Save.

9. Restart Word.

The changes will take effect the next time you open Word and choose Browse Web from the File menu.

In this lesson, you learned how to customize your copy of Internet Assistant to suit your own tastes. In the next lesson, you'll learn how to use the Internet Assistant Help file.

Lesson 20

Using the Internet Assistant Help File

In this lesson, you'll learn how to use the helpful charts and tables in the Internet Assistant Help file.

Viewing the Help File

A standard part of most applications, the Help file can be a great tool for users of a software package. Microsoft's capability to create good Help files has encouraged many other software developers to do the same. Today, most commercial software comes with an entire user's manual online in the form of a Help file. Internet Assistant is no exception.

To view the Help file for Internet Assistant:

1. Start Word.

2. Open the File menu and select the Browse Web command. You are now in Web Browse view.

3. Open the Help menu and select Internet Assistant for Word Help. You see the Help file pictured in Figure 20.1.

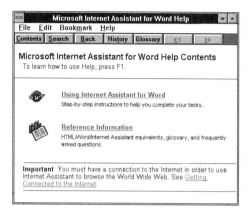

Figure 20.1   The Internet Assistant Help File main screen.

When you first open the Help file, you see two main sections. To open either of these sections, click a title.

In the first section, Using Internet Assistant for Word, you'll find discussions and brief summaries of most of the information covered in this book. If you need quick help on any of these topics, the Help file is only a mouse click away. If you need a more thorough walk-through of a specific topic, use this book as a reference.

To find a topic in the Help file:

1. Be certain that you are in Web Browse view or HTML Edit view.

2. Open the Help menu and select the Internet Assistant for Word Help command. You see the main Help screen, as shown in Figure 20.1.

3. Click the Search button located underneath the menu bar. You see the Search dialog box, as shown in Figure 20.2.

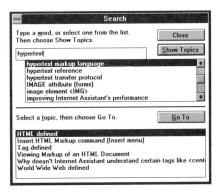

Figure 20.2   The Search dialog box allows you to search for information.

4. Type a word that relates to the topic you need help on (the example shows **hypertext**). The list underneath will match what you typed.

5. Click Show Topics. The list at the bottom will show the list of topics that correspond to your keyword.

6. Highlight the topic that interests you. For this example, you can highlight HTML defined.

7. Click Go To to close the dialog box and display the Help page for the topic you've chosen.

For advanced users, there is the Reference Information section that contains some reference information not covered in this book. Here's a quick look at what you'll find in this section:

- **HTML/Word Equivalents**   Includes a listing of HTML 2.0 Tags and equivalent Word commands and an explanation of what is lost when Word documents are converted to HTML.

- **Menu Commands**   Includes a listing of Internet Assistant Menu Commands.

- **Overviews**   Includes HyperLink Command Overview, Picture Command Overview, and Form Overview.

- **Definitions and Common Questions**   Includes a Glossary and a list of Frequently Asked Questions.

Using the Tables in the Help File

If you are quite familiar with HTML, the Help file contains a table of HTML tags and equivalent Word commands that will help you use Word as an HTML publishing tool.

To get to this table:

1. Start Word.

2. Open the File menu and select Browse Web. You are now in Web Browse view.

3. Open the Help menu and select Internet Assistant for Word Help. The main Help screen for Internet Assistant appears, as shown in Figure 20.1.

4. Click Reference Information. You see the screen shown in Figure 20.3.

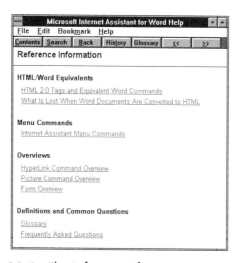

Figure 20.3 The Reference Information screen.

5. Select HTML 2.0 Tags and Equivalent Word Commands. The HTML 2.0 Tag Table appears.

Using the Charts in the Help File

The Help file also contains a brief but thorough description of each of the new menu items added to Word when you install Internet Assistant. To find these charts:

1. Start Word.

2. Open the File menu and select Browse Web. You are now in Web Browse view.

3. Open the Help menu and select Internet Assistant for Word Help. The main Help screen for Internet Assistant appears, as shown in Figure 20.1.

4. Select Reference Information. You see the screen shown in Figure 20.3.

5. Select Internet Assistant Menu Commands. You see two other options:

Menu Commands in Web Browse View

Menu Commands in HTML Edit View

6. Click the option that corresponds to the view you're using. You see a chart that explains each of the new commands.

Using Other Tools in the Help File

For an overview of terminology used in Web browsing and HTML, see the Glossary. To get to the Glossary:

1. Start Word.

2. Open the File menu and select Browse Web. You are now in Web Browse view.

3. Open the Help menu and select Internet Assistant for Word Help. The main Help screen for Internet Assistant appears, as shown in Figure 20.1.

4. Select Reference Information. You see the screen shown in Figure 20.3.

5. Select Glossary. Each word in the Glossary appears as a hyperlink in the Help file. Click a word to see its meaning.

Microsoft also provides a FAQ (Frequently Asked Questions) for Internet Assistant. If you have a question about Internet Assistant (specifically, technical questions), read through this page first. Your question is likely to be here. This will save you time and money, instead of contacting Microsoft directly. To get to the FAQ:

1. Start Word.

2. Open the File menu and select Browse Web. You are now in Web Browse view.

3. Open the Help menu and select Internet Assistant for Word Help. The main Help screen for Internet Assistant appears, as shown in Figure 20.1.

4. Select Reference Information. You see the screen shown in Figure 20.3.

5. Select Frequently Asked Questions. You see a list of common questions and an answer for each one.

6. Each question has a hyperlink following it. Click the word ANSWER to see the answer to the question.

In this lesson, you learned about the helpful charts and tables in the Internet Assistant Help file. In the next lesson, you'll learn some tricks to work with Internet Assistant more efficiently.

Using Internet Assistant Most Efficiently

In this lesson, you'll learn how to use Internet Assistant with other Internet tools, how to speed up Internet Assistant, and how to configure Internet Assistant for proxy servers.

Using Internet Assistant with Other Tools

Internet Assistant, like most software packages, performs many tasks—some well, some not so well. If you've read through the lessons, you should have a very good idea of what Internet Assistant can do for you and how to use the various features. With that in mind, there are certain situations in which you'd be better off to use a different tool.

Internet Assistant is, of course, first and foremost an HTML publishing tool. Its design lends itself to the creation and editing of HTML documents. However, it doesn't support all of the possibilities of HTML. Therefore, it is still a good idea to explore other HTML editors. I use the applet Notepad (which comes with Windows) for most of my advanced HTML writing (fine-tuning, and so on). As a simple, straightforward text editor, it does the job well.

What Advanced HTML?   Internet Assistant only supports HTML specifications through version 2.0 of HTML. However, several enhanced (although not standardized) versions of HTML (such as HTML and HTML 3.0) exist. In order to use them, you must add the code manually. If you're not familiar with other versions of HTML, Internet Assistant will suit you fine, and Notepad will not be necessary.

You've also learned about the good performance of Internet Assistant when printing Web documents. Because Internet Assistant uses Microsoft Word graphics filters (based on your current printer), it can print Web documents remarkably well. However, it can take quite a bit of time to download them.

To speed up this process, use another browser (I use Netscape, but there are many different browsers available) to do your Web browsing. Once you find a document you want to capture for printing or editing or to use in your own document, write down the URL (or copy it to the Clipboard), and then switch to Internet Assistant and download just that page. Using this procedure, you can save tons of time in some cases.

Cut and Paste URLs!   If you're using Netscape or Mosaic (and most other browsers), you can highlight the URL of the current document. Then press Ctrl+C on your keyboard. This will copy the current URL to the Clipboard. After clicking the URL button in Internet Assistant, instead of typing the URL, press Ctrl+V on your keyboard. This will paste the URL into the dialog box. Then press Enter, and the document will begin to download.

Improving the Speed of Internet Assistant

Microsoft Word for Windows is a large and very powerful program, and powerful and fast don't usually work together. Therefore, like most Word users, you've probably noticed that Word runs rather slowly.

Since Internet Assistant is an add-on for Word, you'll notice the same performance problems with it as you do for Word. You can improve the performance of Internet Assistant in several ways:

- Open the View menu and select the Load Images command to toggle off this option. You won't be able to see inline graphics anymore, but downloading pages won't take as long.

- Open the View menu and select Full Screen. You should see just your Web document covering the entire screen. This feature isn't available in many browsers.

- Close down any other applications that might be running.

- Be certain that your system meets the minimum requirements listed in Lesson 3.

Configuring Internet Assistant for Proxy Servers

Proxy servers have a number of different purposes, depending upon your specific system and configuration. With Internet Assistant, proxy servers will most likely be used to get around *firewalls* in the system. If the firewall doesn't allow communication between your machine and the outside (for security purposes), you'll have to have another machine get the information for you, and then send it to your machine. This other machine is known as a proxy server.

Firewall   A machine or series of machines connected and configured to keep hackers out of the system. In most cases, incoming traffic must clear each of these machines before being allowed in.

If you're not familiar with proxy servers, then you won't need to read this section. If you are in a corporate environment, your system administrator should take care of this configuration. If you are the system administrator and you need to use proxy servers, this section is for you. Most users, however, will not need to configure Internet Assistant for proxy servers.

To configure Internet Assistant for use with proxy servers:

1. Open the File menu and select Open. The Open dialog box appears.

2. Double-click your Windows directory in the Directories box. You may have to double-click the root directory first.

3. Check the Confirm Conversion option in the lower right-hand corner of the Open dialog box.

4. Type **iwia.ini** in the File Name box and click OK. You see the Confirm Conversions dialog box.

5. Select Text Only and click OK. The .INI file appears on-screen at this point.

6. Find the [Proxy Servers] section.

7. Fill in the network address and the port of the servers you want to use as proxies. Your network administrator should have this information.

8. Open the File menu and select Save.

9. Restart Word.

Internet Assistant should work with your proxy servers after you restart Word.

In this lesson, you learned how to use Internet Assistant more efficiently. In the following appendixes, you'll find all kinds of helpful information, including popular Web sites with lots of information on various topics.

Appendix

Interesting Web Sites

I've been using the World Wide Web for quite some time, and I've found a number of different sites that contain useful, interesting, or entertaining information. I've included a list of some of them here.

Each entry starts with the URL. (See Lesson 6 for more information about what an URL is.) You can type an URL into the Open URL dialog in Internet Assistant. See Lesson 6 for more information on how to download a Web document (browse the Web) with Internet Assistant.

Watch for Capitalization! In most cases, you need to type these URLs *exactly* as you see them here. This includes the correct upper- and lowercase letters.

http://www.w3.org/hypertext/DataSources Top.html   A general overview of the Web. This is a great starting-points document for the beginning Web user. If you're new to Web browsing, start here.

http://arts.usf.edu   The University of South Florida College of Fine Arts, with over 500 students, is home to the Art, Dance, and Theatre Departments, and the School of Music, as well as the USF Contemporary Art Museum and Graphic studio.

http://gallery.sjsu.edu   This is the World Wide Web server for the Art Department at San Jose State University. You can find information about art shows and some interesting facts about new artists.

http://www.westga.edu/~coop   This is JOBNET, a collection of job-related resources scattered across the Internet that have been collected from various sources. Sources used include Gopher, Usenet News, and the World Wide Web.

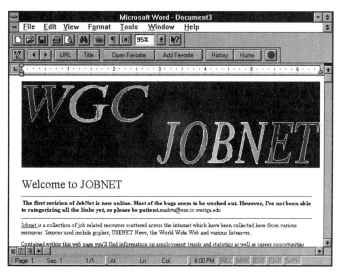

Figure A.1   JOBNET.

http://www.careermag.com/careermag   The network world has career opportunities, whether you are changing positions or building contacts and ideas for the future. *Career Magazine* is a comprehensive resource, designed to meet the individual needs of networked job seekers. You can return to *Career Magazine* for valuable new information every day. Put *Career Magazine*'s URL into your Favorites document and begin your networked career search.

http://web.fie.com   This is the Federal Information Exchange, facilitating a partnership of 10 federal agencies under the leadership of the Department of Energy. Today, Federal Information Exchange's FEDIX/MOLIS On-Line Information System has 125,000+ users. Be sure to check out FEDIX, which contains federal agency opportunity information.

http://www.pathfinder.com/pathfinder/Greet.html This is Time Warner. This page contains links to most of Time's publications, including *TIME*, *Sports Illustrated*, *People*, *Money*, and others.

http://www.dbisna.com   This is Dun and Bradstreet. You can find information on market research, management, and other financial topics.

http://www.tti.com   This is Citibank, the largest and most innovative financial service provider in the United States.

http://meta.stanford.edu/quotes.html   This is a killer collection of great one-liners.

http://www.brandonu.ca/~ennsnr/Tags   Tag lines, more tag lines, and even more tag lines. There are currently 49,358 tag lines in this collection.

http://www.msstate.edu/Movies   The Internet Movie Database at Mississippi State University. Great for movie reviews and information on actors and actresses.

http://www.music.fsu.edu/ftp.html   Music instruction software, sounds, and pictures, which also shows a nice example of using inline graphics as bullets for a list.

http://www.shopping2000.com:80/shopping2000/tower The Tower Records home page, which contains a link to a searchable database of the entire Tower catalog. Great for gifts and that hard-to-find LP.

http://www.music.sony.com This is Sony online; a great page with lots of killer links, but very graphics intensive. This page could take awhile to download with Internet Assistant.

http://webcrawler.cs.washington.edu/WebCrawler This is the WebCrawler I talked about in Lesson 6. The WebCrawler is one of the best searching tools available today.

http://www.att.net/dir800 This AT&T 800 Directory on the Internet is one more value-added service from your friends at AT&T. Keep this one in your Favorites document, but remember to read the copyright notice.

http://www.microsoft.com The Microsoft home page, which contains links to great information about Microsoft's upcoming products, including Windows 95. You'll even find Microsoft employment opportunities.

http://www.compuserve.com CompuServe, of course. You'll find links to a CompuServe overview, CompuServe press releases, MultiMedia, and CompuServe Internet Services.

http://www.bsdi.com Berkeley Software Design, Inc., the makers of BSD UNIX. This is a great-looking Web page that demonstrates the effect of colorful lists. This page contains many links to tons of great information about the company plus current issues and discussions about the operating system.

http://www.intel.com The folks who made my Pentium. These pages are easily among the most attractive I've ever seen. Browse for current press releases and information on Intel products. Notice the carefully placed graphics and subtle shading.

http://www.creaf.com   Creative Labs, Inc., based in Milpitas, California, is the leader in PC sound, video, and CD-ROM multimedia solutions, with Sound Blaster setting the industry standard for sound on PC-based platforms. Creative Labs, Inc. develops, manufactures, and markets a family of multimedia sound and video products and a range of multi-media kits for entertainment, education, and productivity markets. This Web page provides information about Creative's product line.

http://www.sprintlink.net   SprintLink is a commercial Internet service provider; this site offers information about current products and services.

http://www.netscape.com   This is Netscape Communica-tions, Inc., makers of the Netscape Web browser and NetSite Web server. Arguably, Netscape is the finest Internet tech-nology available to the consumer today. If you're looking for a Web browser, this is the place to go.

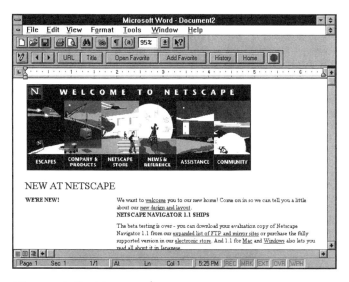

Figure A.2   Netscape home page.

http://www.sun.com   This is the home page for Sun Microsystems, makers of UNIX Workstations, Solaris, and much more. Check out the Technology & Research link for some very interesting information.

http://www.cray.com   This is Cray Research. They make incredibly powerful computers that cost several million dollars apiece. Find out more about the leading edge of supercomputing technology as well.

http://www.ibm.com/   I'm sure you've heard of these folks. They're IBM. Get information about IBM's market performance and new product releases.

http://www.apple.com   Downloading this page may take awhile. The graphics are quite large, and there are a lot of them. This Web page contains many great images and tons of information about Apple and Apple products.

http://www.dell.com   Dell Computer Corporation designs, develops, manufactures, markets, services, and supports a complete line of personal computers compatible with industry standards. This page is also rather graphics intensive. You'll find information on Dell's extensive product line.

http://www.xerox.com   A very extensive online database of Xerox information, from product announcements to press releases to links to XSoft, the software division of Xerox.

http://www.vegas.com   It's all here. Great information about the town, including tips on how to spend lots of money! No bets online, though.

http://tns-www.lcs.mit.edu/cgi-bin/sports   Up-to-date and complete coverage of your favorite teams and sports issues. A must for the Internet-surfing sports fan.

http://www.tvnet.com/UTVL/utvl.html   This page contains links to hundreds of pages concerning hundreds of popular TV shows, past and present.

http://www.cgl.com/~it   Use this URL to get information about international flights, domestic flights, tours, cruises, and travel news.

http://www.commerce.net   CommerceNet is a not-for-profit mutual benefit corporation that is conducting the first large-scale market trial of technologies and business processes to support electronic commerce via the Internet. You can find all kinds of information about the prospect of electronic commerce via the Internet.

http://www.directory.net   A directory of commercial services, products, and information available on the Internet.

https://www.internet.net   The Internet Shopping Network. You can join the ISN and shop for products and services via the Internet.

http://www.quote.com   Quote.Com is a service dedicated to providing quality financial market data to the Internet community. This includes current quotes on stocks, commodity futures, mutual funds, and bonds. It also includes business news, market analysis and commentary, fundamental (balance sheet) data, and company profiles.

http://www.acm.uiuc.edu/rml/govt.html   This page contains links to the major branches of the United States government and loads of information about each one.

http://branch.com   Branch Mall. A shopping mall on the Internet. Use this URL to access tons of information and thousands of vendors on the Internet.

http://www.comdex.com:8000   COMDEX, a computer convention, maintains this page. Use it to get information about upcoming COMDEX events or to register for the show.

http://www.yellow.com   The World Wide Web Yellow Pages. Use this URL to search for countless vendors, service providers, and news resources on the Internet.

http://www.ncsa.uiuc.edu/SDG/Software/Mosaic /Docs/whats-new.html   What's new on the Web. This constantly changing page, courtesy of NCSA, contains links to new resources and information that affects many Internet users. Consult this URL weekly.

Appendix

Glossary

add-on   A program, utility, or software package feature that doesn't ship with the product. Software companies usually produce add-ons after creating the software and provide them to registered users for a small fee. Internet Assistant is an add-on to Microsoft Word, and, unlike other add-ons, is free to registered users of Word.

anonymous FTP   A method of accessing files on a system without needing to have an account on that system.

binary file   A file that is usually a program or a compressed data file. Binary files can't be read or understood by people.

cache   A temporary storage area in memory. Internet Assistant uses a cache to improve the speed of retrieving documents you've already viewed.

CGI (Common Gateway Interface)   A specification for external programs (such as Web browsers) to interact with servers (such as Web servers).

Clipboard   An area of memory set aside by Windows that you can use to copy data and information from one application or document to another.

client   The software and computer you use at your workstation. The client connects to a server at a remote location.

domain name   A naming scheme used by the Internet to allow people to easily identify a specific computer. Each domain name represents a numerical address. A separate computer translates the domain name into the numerical address (known as an IP address) for you (like the phone book converts a person's name into a phone number).

download   To transfer a file from a remote computer to your computer.

e-mail   Electronic mail. A method of sending typed notes or letters across a computer network. Some companies have e-mail that works within the company. It is also possible to use the Internet to send e-mail.

FAQ   Frequently Asked Questions. A text file containing common questions and answers about a product or procedure. You'll find a FAQ for Internet Assistant in the Help file.

Favorites document   A user-configured list of your favorite Web pages.

FTP   File transfer protocol. A program that enables you to connect to a remote system over the network and transfer files to and from that system.

fill-out forms   Fill-out forms give the user of a Web document the ability to send information to the server. You can use forms to register software, request information, and even order pizza. Many Web sites also use forms as a way to search for specific information on the computer. You can also use forms to create custom Web pages on the fly.

firewall   A computer or series of computers connected and configured to keep hackers out of the system. In most cases, incoming traffic must clear each of these computers before being allowed in.

Gopher   A first-generation browsing system that gives you access to resources linked together by a menu system. This technology is being replaced, for the most part, by the World Wide Web.

gopherspace   A large collection of menus that point to other menus and text files. You can browse through these menus and text files to gopher to (find) all kinds of information.

history list   A file containing the URLs of the last 50 documents you viewed in Web Browse view. You can change the default number of documents to something other than 50 (see Lesson 19).

home page   A starting place. A home page can be the starting document used by a Web browser or the starting-points document on a Web site.

horizontal rule   A thick, black horizontal line that separates sections of a document.

host   A remote system or server.

HTML   HyperText Markup Language. Web documents are composed using this language. Internet Assistant automatically generates the code for this language, saving you countless hours in Web page development.

HTML editor   A software package or utility designed to assist you in writing HTML documents. Although you can write HTML documents in any text editor or word processor, an HTML editor usually contains some extra features that make your job a bit easier.

HTTP   HyperText Transport Protocol. This is the computer language Internet Assistant and other Web browsers use to transfer documents from a server to your local PC.

hyperlink   A word, phrase, or picture that points to another resource or document.

hypertext   A technology that links network resources together. Each resource contains hyperlinks to other resources.

inline graphic   A picture that appears within an HTML document. You cannot use some graphics within a document; you must view them with a separate program.

Internet service provider A company that provides access to the Internet via a phone line or dedicated connection.

Local area network (LAN) A collection of computers (usually in the same building) connected together with some type of wire. The computers on this network all use the same computer language to share information.

local web A series of interconnected Word documents that behave similarly to the World Wide Web. Rather than scattered around the world, the collection of documents resides on a single local server.

NCSA National Center for Supercomputing Applications. This group designed Mosaic, the first graphical Web browser.

patch A small program that updates or changes another program. Patches usually fix bugs (minor program flaws) or add features. Installing the Word 6.0a patch enables you to run Internet Assistant if you have Word 6.0.

PPP Point-to-Point Protocol. Compared to SLIP, this is a newer (but less common) method of using Internet over a modem. PPP automatically takes care of much of the setup, and therefore it is much easier for nontechnical people to use.

protocol A computer language for exchanging data between remote hosts and local systems. Each type of resource on the Internet uses a different protocol.

search engine A program that searches through data (such as Web pages) for information and sends the user results (such as which Web pages contain information about fish).

server A computer on the Internet that stores documents or information and runs a program that communicates with remote computers to share information. A server that runs software for WWW users to connect to is a Web server or Web site.

SLIP   Serial Line Internet Protocol. An older method of using the Internet over a modem (or a serial cable). Most Internet service providers allow SLIP access.

Telnet   Terminal emulation link network. Telnet allows you to connect to a system from a remote location and operate the system as if it were local.

TCP/IP   Transport Control Protocol/Internet Protocol. These two computer languages allow the Internet to work.

UNIX   A predominantly free operating system used extensively on the Internet.

URL   Uniform Resource Locator. A special method of specifying different types of resources on the Internet in a similar format. The URL makes it possible for one application to retrieve many types of documents because each URL is an "address" to a specific document or menu.

Usenet   A collection of newsgroups (discussion groups) stored in a central location. Newsgroups are similar to message areas on BBS systems, forums on CompuServe, or the employee bulletin board at work where people can post items of interest for others to read. You can connect to a computer and read through the articles in a specific newsgroup or contribute new articles to that newsgroup.

WAIS   Wide Area Information Search. A complex search engine that locates information resources on the Internet by means of a scoring system. Each resource is "weighted" based on the search criteria. The computer then presents you with the results of the search.

.WAV file   A compressed file that contains a digitized sound or recording.

Web site   A computer that contains a collection of Web pages.

Wide area network   A network of networks; usually several LANs (local area networks) connected together. The Internet is an example of a wide area network.

World Wide Web (WWW)   A complex collection of graphical documents stored on thousands of computers around the world. Each document is connected to other documents via hypertext links.

Index